DATE DUE

Education i
the People'
and U.S.-Cl
Exchanges

Linda A. R

NAFSA
National Association for Foreign Student Affairs
Washington, D.C.

LINDA A. REED is executive director of the Council on Standards for International Educational Travel and a private consultant on U.S.-China educational affairs.

The National Association for Foreign Student Affairs (NAFSA) is a nonprofit membership association that provides training, information, and other educational services to professionals in the field of international educational exchange. Its 5,800 members—from every state in the United States and more than 50 other countries—represent primarily colleges and universities but also elementary and secondary schools, public and private educational associations, exchange organizations, national and international corporations and foundations, and community organizations. Through its publications, workshops, consultations with institutions, and conferences, the association serves as a source of professional training, a reference for standards of performance, and an advocate for the most effective operation of international educational exchange.

Library of Congress Cataloging-in-Publication Data

Reed, Linda A.
    Education in the People's Republic of China and U.S.-China educational exchange.

    Rev. and expanded ed. of: An introduction to education in the People's Republic of China and U.S.-China educational exchanges / Thomas Fingar, Linda A. Reed. c1982.
    Bibliography: p.
    1. Educational exchanges—United States. 2. Educational exchanges—China. 3. Education—China. I. Fingar, Thomas. An introduction to education in the People's Republic of China and U.S.-China educational exchanges. II. Title.
LB2285.C55R44   1988   370.19'6'0951   88-34476
ISBN 0-912207-42-6

Contents

Preface and Acknowledgments

In the six years that have elapsed since publication of the revised edition of *Introduction to Education in the People's Republic of China and U.S.-China Educational Exchanges,* the number of Chinese students and scholars on U.S. campuses has grown from approximately 7,000 to over 25,000 students and as many as 5,000 scholars in non-degree programs.* During the same period, the number of Americans teaching, studying, or conducting research in China at any one time has increased from 200 to 1,000 during the normal academic year and to as many as 2,500 during the summer, when students participate in short-term Chinese language programs. As important as these increases are, they would not in themselves have required the extensive revisions that occasion a new publication.

Why the need for a new, thoroughly revised publication? Foremost, the Chinese government in 1985 and 1986 issued major documents that redefine the goals of the country's educational policy in important ways. As part of the expansion and reform of the educational system, the number of institutions of higher learning in China has increased from 704 to 1,063, while the number of students enrolled in these institutions has increased by more than a third to some two million. An additional 1.8 million students enrolled in television universities and other special courses. Curricula have changed, with the social sciences and humanities now receiving greater emphasis than before. Graduate enrollments have more than doubled. Undergraduate degrees were conferred for the first time in 1982 (graduate degrees were first conferred in 1981).

In addition, a great deal more is known now about education in the PRC than was the case six years ago. The increased knowledge derives in part from both quantitative and qualitative improvements in the information that is made available by agencies of the Chinese government and by individual schools and research institutes. It also arises from the exchange process itself: more people have spent extended periods in China, and Chinese citizens on U.S. campuses now come from a much wider variety of institutions than was the case several years ago.

---

* As used in this publication, the terms China and Chinese apply only to the mainland provinces of the People's Republic of China and their residents.

Other factors contributing to the need for this work include the changing composition of those applying and arriving from the PRC, changes in U.S. and Chinese laws and official procedures, and the way in which exchanges have evolved. This publication includes much new information about Chinese and U.S. government changes in policies and regulations that affect U.S.-China educational exchanges.

Despite additions, refinements, and—hopefully—improvements to earlier volumes, this new work has the same basic goals and requires the same qualification as did the original *Introduction* produced in 1979 by the U.S.-China Education Clearinghouse. It is worth quoting from the Foreword to that first edition:

> This *Introduction* is not intended as a definitive analysis either of China's educational system and policies or of the exchange process to date. It aims, rather, to provide background information which we hope will be of use to American educators and educational administrators in managing their exchange relationship with the People's Republic of China.

Part One of the present work reviews how the changing political atmosphere in China during the past 100 years has affected the country's educational practices. It describes the organization of the present-day education system in China, including the selection procedures and program offerings of institutions of higher education. Part Two is an overview of U.S.-China educational exchanges to date. Part Three constitutes a practical guide for admissions officers, foreign student advisers, and others who work with Chinese students and scholars on a daily basis.

The first two editions of the *Introduction* were produced by the U.S.-China Education Clearinghouse, a joint project of the National Association for Foreign Student Affairs (NAFSA) and the Committee on Scholarly Communication with the People's Republic of China (CSCPRC) that was funded by the U.S. Information Agency (then the U.S. International Communication Agency). The clearinghouse existed from October 1979 through April 1982 to gather information about education in China, to disseminate this information to U.S. institutions of higher education and other interested parties, and to monitor U.S.-China educational exchanges. Since the end of the clearinghouse, NAFSA has continued to disseminate the publications produced by the clearinghouse, produce updates to and revisions of those publications, and monitor U.S.-China educational exchanges.

During the first year of the clearinghouse project, Dr. Pierre M. Perrolle was the person at the CSCPRC responsible for clearinghouse activities. Dr. Perrolle coauthored the first edition of the *Introduction* and contributed to subsequent clearinghouse publications through the creation of valuable files and the sharing of insights and information. I wish to acknowledge his role and thank him for helping the clearinghouse realize the goals that were set at its inception.

Much of the material in Part One of the new work and of the 1982 revision is based on or excerpted from *Higher Education in the People's Republic of China,* edited by Thomas Fingar (Stanford University, 1980). For permission to republish portions of that report, I thank Stanford's Northeast Asia-United States Forum on International Policy. Dr. Fingar himself, however, needs to receive particular acknowledgment and thanks. He was the person at the CSCPRC responsible for clearinghouse activities after Dr. Perrolle left, and he and I worked together to produce seven of the ten clearinghouse publications. He remained an invaluable source of information after his return to Stanford's Northeast Asia-United States Forum on International Policy, and has continued to be such in his current position with the U.S. Department of State and as a member of NAFSA's Advisory Committee on U.S.-China Educational Exchanges.

The State Education Commission of China offered invaluable assistance by providing a great deal of information about aspects of education in China through its series of brochures entitled "A Glimpse of Education in China" that was produced in 1986.

I also wish to acknowledge and thank the following persons for their contributions to and review of this publication:

Robert Brashear, State Education Commission of China
Sarah Briggs, University of Michigan
Archer Brown, National Association for Foreign Student Affairs
Karlene Dickey, Stanford University
Richard Getrich, National Association for Foreign Student Affairs
Eleanor Harris, U.S. Department of State
Jay Henderson, Institute of International Education—Southeast Asia Office
Mary Hitt, U.S. Information Agency
Gail Hochhauser, Consortium for International Cooperation in Higher Education
Leo Orleans, Library of Congress
McKinney Russell, U.S. Embassy, Beijing
Glenn Shive, Institute of International Education—China Programs
Karen Stanton, U.S. Embassy, Beijing
Ruizhong Wang, Embassy of the People's Republic of China
Russell Webster, Educational Testing Service
Geoffrey Wood, University of Pittsburgh
Yigu Yuan, Embassy of the People's Republic of China

In addition, I wish to thank Melanie Moreau, Elizabeth Sedlins, and Sarah Herr of NAFSA for their efficient and accurate assistance in preparing this publication.

Finally, on behalf of NAFSA, I wish to extend appreciation and thanks to the Student Support Services Division of the U.S. Information Agency for providing the support that made this publication possible.

The views in this publication are not necessarily those of NAFSA or of the U.S. Information Agency. Any inaccuracies of fact or interpretation are the responsibility of the author.

It has been a pleasure for staff and members of the National Association for Foreign Student Affairs to work with the exceptional Chinese students and scholars who have come to U.S. institutions and with colleagues at the Chinese Embassy and consulates in the United States and at the State Education Commission and institutions of higher education in China. It is hoped that the materials collected and disseminated by the U.S.-China Education Clearinghouse and NAFSA have been and will continue to be of assistance in facilitating the educational exchange process between the United States and China.

LINDA A. REED

Washington, DC
Fall 1988

PART ONE

Education in the People's Republic of China

China's 1.1 million regular schools, 9.7 million teachers, and 202.6 million full-time students constitute the world's largest school system. In addition, there are more than 227,000 adult education schools with 355,800 teachers and 25.8 million students. Indeed, the numbers are so large that it is useful to view them in comparative perspective: in 1985, the total population of the United States was 238.7 million; Florida, the seventh most populous state, had 9.7 million residents. Twelve U.S. states, plus the District of Columbia, have fewer people than China has schools. As awesome and important as these aggregate figures are, they tell only part of the story; to appreciate the condition, complexity, and challenges of education in China, it is necessary to consider a number of additional facts and figures:

- Of the 204 million students, 134 million are in grades one through six; only two million are enrolled in colleges and universities.
- Many classroom teachers have had only rudimentary formal train-

ing; it will take years, perhaps decades, to reach desired levels of preparation (e.g., ensuring that all primary school teachers have at least the equivalent of a middle-school education).

- Despite huge enrollments, China is a long way from its announced goal of nine years of compulsory education—six primary and three junior-middle; in October 1985, only one-third of China's counties had made primary education universal.
- Schools and the quality of instruction vary enormously; although the overall quality is rather low, some students receive an excellent education.

Although large numbers and certain features of China's educational system (described in the pages that follow) create a number of political, pedagogical, and financial difficulties, they also produce a number of positive consequences germane to a discussion of student exchanges. For example, officially sponsored student applicants from China are selected through a highly competitive achievement-based process. Of the approximately seven million young people who graduate from senior middle-school each year, only 600,000 go on to college. Of the nearly 500,000 students who graduate from colleges or universities each year, approximately 45,000 enter graduate programs. Early in 1985, the Chinese government announced its intentions of increasing the number of state-financed students going abroad for studies each year from 3,000 to 4,000. With such a large initial pool and rigorous adherence to high standards of quality, the ability of those who pass each successive selection process is high.

Chapters 3–6 describe the education system that exists in China today. However, in order to understand the origins, capacity, and objectives of this system, it is useful to review, albeit in very brief fashion, its traditional and twentieth-century precursors. In the interest of brevity and relevance, the descriptions of the past will focus on recurring themes, contrasting approaches, and tertiary-level instruction.

1
The Evolution of China's Education System

Traditional (Pre-1905)

Respect for education was reputedly the hallmark of traditional China. Though exaggerated and incomplete, this stereotypical characterization is essentially correct. Scholar-officials were highly venerated and idolized by ambitious youth throughout the country. To ascend the ranks of officialdom, one had to pass a series of exacting examinations administered by the central government. These examinations were designed to determine mastery of a specific corpus of knowledge—the "classics." The number passing the examinations was limited by national and provincial quotas and never constituted more than a tiny percentage of the total population.

Although the government used the examinations to recruit able officials and promoted the idea that anyone who studied diligently could compete successfully for scholarly degrees and the resultant wealth and power, it provided little or no direct support for education. There were no public schools, and the cost of attending one of the better private academies was far beyond the reach of most citizens. Individuals could study on their own, and there were less expensive schools, but the fact remained that to be truly competitive it was almost imperative to attend one of the expensive academies. Education was highly valued but difficult to achieve.

The academies and less formal programs that prepared young men to take the official examinations required students to memorize vast amounts of material (such as poetry, philosophy, and literary commentaries); they provided no instruction in technical or "practical" subjects. During the latter half of the nineteenth century, officials began to perceive that the lack of technical training and the resultant technological and military weakness had put China at a severe disadvantage in the intensifying competition with Western nations. To remedy this situation, they founded a number of new or "modern"

3

schools that taught foreign languages, science, and engineering subjects. Because they did not prepare students for the civil service examinations that were the key to official careers, however, the new schools were widely regarded as second-class institutions. Many of the new schools were further stigmatized by their association with foreign missionaries and by the fact that graduates, almost by definition, did not subscribe to the common set of values regarded as critical to the preservation of traditional social, political, and economic relationships.

As the skills possessed by graduates of the modern schools became more important—especially against the background of national disintegration that had begun in the mid-nineteenth century—classically trained officials became increasingly uneasy about the stability of the system of which they were a part and about the "loyalty" of the younger technocrats with practical or Western knowledge. Tension between defenders of the status quo and those with a different vision of China's future contributed to the formation of revolutionary groups and the determination of some provincial and municipal officials to take control of, and hence responsibility for, the emerging system of education.

Building a "Modern" System (1905-49)

The evolution of China's education system entered a new stage in 1905 with abolition of the traditional civil service examination and establishment of the first Ministry of Education. The demise of the examination system was fatal to the traditional academies and the career aspirations of those who had prepared to become scholar-officials. At the same time, it opened a broad range of new positions to those with practical skills and modern—Western—learning. Previously viewed as inferior, the modern schools became the key to personal advancement and national self-strengthening efforts. Because they were deemed so important to China's future, these schools had to be supported and controlled by the central government. Central control, to be exercised through the Ministry of Education, was intended to ensure both the quality of instruction and the loyalty of those in the system.

Civil war and foreign invasion impeded development of a national system of education during the half century prior to the founding of the People's Republic of China on October 1, 1949, but there were substantial achievements. A variety of colleges and universities, many established and supported by missionary organizations, offered instruction in a wide range of disciplines and technical specialities. There were a small number of graduate programs, but most students seeking advanced training went abroad to study.

The belief that science was the basis for all investigation and the pressing need for engineers and technical specialists led to both an emphasis on science and technology and a tendency toward early and narrow specialization. These tendencies were most pronounced at the tertiary level, but were also evident in secondary schools. Below the tertiary level, however, the most important task of the education system was to inculcate values important to the modernization of China—patriotism, loyalty to the government, respect for authority, diligence, thrift, etc. Civics or "moral education" was an important part of the curriculum.

Although Communist officials have continually denigrated the quality, size, and offerings of the system they inherited, its legacy was far from trivial. According to their own statistics, there were 340,000 primary schools, 4,000 middle schools, and 200 universities and colleges at the time of national liberation in 1949. These schools, and many of the teachers trained before 1949, have been the foundation of the present education system.

Restoration, Reform, and Expansion (1949-66)

Like their Nationalist predecessors, the Communist officials who took power in 1949 regarded the education system as critical to the success of their effort to transform China. Accordingly, they immediately set out to restore and transform the schools. The return of peace made it possible to enroll more students and to refurbish classrooms, libraries, and laboratories. Teaching techniques and materials developed in Communist base areas in the 1940s were introduced throughout the country. Major transformation of the system, however, had to await rehabilitation of existing facilities and formulation of overall plans and policies.

Beginning in 1952–53, China adopted the education system that had been developed in the Soviet Union. Many elements of the Soviet approach (e.g., emphasis on science and technology, early and narrow specialization, and central control of the school system and curricula) also were part of the Chinese system that had evolved since 1905. Others were new, such as reorganization of existing schools and creation of new colleges and universities to achieve greater institutional specialization, the establishment of separate research institutes under the Academy of Sciences and various ministries other than the Ministry of Education, and the establishment (and/or assignment) of secondary schools subordinate to production ministries with the goal of training workers for particular industries.

Enrollments in primary and secondary schools increased steadily and the quality of instruction improved as new teachers were trained and more materials, many of them translated from Russian originals, were made available. College enrollments also increased, but at a much slower rate. Selection was based primarily on academic achievement as demonstrated by performance on standardized examinations. The desire to concentrate resources to ensure high quality while simultaneously expanding enrollment opportunities led to the creation of a hierarchy of schools at all levels of the system. "Key" schools were assigned the best teachers and best students, and graduates of these schools were assured the most important positions.

As in preceding decades, thousands of young people went abroad to study; whereas they had previously gone to the West and Japan, they now went to the Soviet Union and Eastern Europe. Perhaps 40,000 Chinese were trained abroad during this period. Chinese colleges and universities concentrated on the training of undergraduates; only some 15,000 to 20,000 graduate students were enrolled prior to 1966.

Cultural Revolution (1966-76)

In mid-1966, China entered a ten-year period of political and social turmoil known as the "Great Proletarian Cultural Revolution," or, in more recent parlance, the "lost decade." Every facet of Chinese society was affected, but the education system suffered the most severe disruption and the most serious long-term consequences. Schools were closed entirely for periods ranging from a few months (in the case of primary and most secondary schools) to several years (colleges did not reopen until 1971–72). When colleges reopened, they were radically different than they had been in the spring of 1966.

Primary and secondary enrollments increased dramatically, but the quality of instruction dropped precipitously because experienced teachers were humiliated and denied permission to teach, virtually all textbooks were withdrawn but not replaced, and classroom discipline evaporated. According to official PRC reports, 160 million young people were victimized by misguided education policies that reversed past emphasis on academic achievement; many of these young people are said to be barely literate.

The impact on higher education was even more serious. When colleges did reopen, four- to six-year programs were reduced to only two to three years, political cant and "practical experience" were substituted for theoretical or substantive courses in science, economics, engineering, or other specialities, and enrollments were based on peer recommendation and "class background" rather than academic achievement. Senior faculty were criticized and often assigned to menial jobs within the universities or in remote locations. Highly trained younger faculty were unable to conduct research, pursue their specialities, or stay abreast of developments in their fields abroad.

Perhaps the easiest way to summarize the changes in the education system that occurred during the Cultural Revolution is to contrast the objectives and practices of that period to those of the preceding decades. Emphasis on science and engineering was displaced by injunctions to study politics and apply the "Thought of Mao Zedong." Centralization and standardization in education were reversed; individual schools and teachers prepared their own materials and local units took responsibility for schools. Concentration of resources and an emphasis on quality gave way to dispersion and pursuit of absolute equality. By and large, education was reduced to the lowest common denominator.

While it is true, as is now acknowledged by Chinese officials, that the country and its education system would pay a heavy price for the misguided policies and unintended consequences of the Cultural Revolution, the situation was not entirely bleak. Some of those selected to attend colleges by peer groups were quite intelligent and did maximize the opportunity to study. Some, perhaps several thousand, youth unable to attend formal classes were tutored by friends or relatives or simply read everything available. But these and other bright spots exist despite, not because of, the measures adopted by the party leaders now derisively labeled the "Gang of Four."

Recovery and Transformation (1977-)

One of the first tasks undertaken in late 1976 by the leaders who assumed power after the death of Mao and purge of the "Gang of Four" was restoration of the educational system that had existed on the eve of the Cultural Revolution. Although the principal features of the present system are described in some detail in Chapters 3–6, they are summarized here.

Academic achievement has been restored as the primary criterion for admission not only to colleges and universities but also to the best middle schools. Studies in support of the Four Modernizations—agriculture, industry, national defense, and science and technology—are preeminent in the curricula of secondary and tertiary schools. On a rotating basis, teachers are being released from classroom duties so they can return to school for additional study. Once compelled to spend endless hours in meetings and "political study," specialists now are assured that they can devote most working hours to their professions. Whereas very few students studied abroad during the Cultural Revolution, thousands now attend classes in Western and Japanese colleges and universities. Graduate training in China has been restored, but the government still sponsors thousands of carefully selected graduate students enrolled in foreign institutions because of limited space in Chinese graduate programs.

Restoration is not the only objective of current policies in education. Gradually, China is beginning to transform the educational system that has evolved over the past several decades. On May 27, 1985, the Central Committee of the Communist Party of China issued a "Decision on the Reform of the Educational Structure," and in April 1986, the Fourth Plenary session of the Sixth National People's Congress approved the Seventh Five-Year Plan (1986–90) for National Economic and Social Development. Both are having a major impact on the educational system. The committee recognized that educational reforms are instrumental in realizing economic reforms. As stated in the Decision, the major problems that needed to be corrected included the following:

1. In the central government: departments in charge of educational administration were exercising too rigid a control over the schools, and, particularly, over the colleges and universities, depriving them of their vitality. These departments also were failing to manage effectively matters that were well within their jurisdiction.

2. In the educational structure: elementary education was deemed inadequate; there were not enough quality schools; there was a serious shortage of qualified teachers and basic facilities; vocational and technical education, which was urgently needed for economic development, had not expanded as expected; there was an indiscriminate arrangement of disciplines and levels of higher education.

3. In ideology, course content, and teaching methods: insufficient attention was being paid to the development of students' ability to think independently and creatively; inadequate efforts were being made to educate students in Marxism; many course textbooks were outdated, teaching methods stereotyped, and practice sessions ignored; specialities offered covered a very limited range of academic subjects; education in China was divorced, to varying degrees, from the needs of economic and social growth and lagged behind the scientific and cultural development of the world as it was in 1985.

To change the situation, the central committee called for a systematic reform of the educational structure that would streamline administration; give units at lower levels responsibility to extend the schools' decision-making power in the administration of school affairs; reform the labor and personnel system; and revise any guidelines, course content, and teaching methods that were at odds with socialist modernization. Through these reforms, the central committee believed that elementary education would be substantially strengthened, vocational and technical education would be greatly expanded, colleges and universities would be able to exploit their potential and exercise their initiative to the full, outside-school and after-school education would develop with regular school education, and education of all kinds and at all levels would address the multiple needs of economic and social development.

It was recognized that education could not be improved without increased funds. So, every year since 1985 and for the foreseeable future, central and local government appropriations for educational purposes have been increasing and will continue to increase at a rate faster than the increase in the state's regular revenues. The average expenditure on education per student also is increasing steadily—the overall amount available to be spent, however, is determined by the growth of the national economy.

Much progress has been made since 1985; for instance, universities now enjoy much greater autonomy than before. However, much remains to be done. Specific reforms are now being implemented in four major areas.

Decentralization and Compulsory Education: entrusting responsibility for elementary education to local authorities and instituting nine-year compulsory education.

Instituting nine-year compulsory education. Nine years of education—six in primary school, three in junior middle-school—is being implemented and is, by law, to be compulsory for all school-age children. Because China is a vast country, with uneven economic and cultural development, the requirements and contents of universally available education vary from place to place. In some cities and economically developed areas in the coastal provinces and the interior, where one-quarter of the country's population resides, junior middle-school education already has become universal. All such areas are expected to make junior middle-school education of the required standard universal by 1990.

Economically semi-developed townships and villages, where one-half of the country's population resides, are striving to make primary school education universal and up to standard. At the same time, they are preparing to make junior middle-school (regular or

9

vocational/technical) education universal by 1995. Economically underdeveloped areas, where one-quarter of the country's population resides, are, as circumstances permit, taking a variety of measures to spread elementary education in varying degrees. State assistance is being provided in educational development, supplementing educational funds raised locally.

Local people's congresses are drawing up regulations concerning compulsory education in light of local conditions and are making decisions on the measures, methods, and deadlines for the enforcement of the nine-year compulsory education system. Simultaneously, pre-school education and special education for the blind, the deaf and mute, the handicapped, and retarded children are being developed.

Building a contingent of qualified and dedicated teachers and taking specific measures to raise status and material benefits of teachers. China has stepped up training for existing teachers and begun assessing their performance. Normal school education is being developed, teacher training is being increased, and correspondence courses, as well as radio and television lessons, are being arranged so that by 1990 the majority of teachers will be qualified for the jobs they hold. After 1990, only those who have received the required schooling or obtained qualification certificates will be allowed to serve as teachers. No government department or any other unit will be allowed to transfer qualified teachers from secondary or primary schools to other jobs.

Decentralizing the power of administration. While central authorities still determine major policies, principles, and overall plans, local authorities now are responsible for drawing up and implementing specific policies, rules and regulations, and plans for guiding, administering, and monitoring the work of schools. The authorities of the provinces, autonomous regions, and centrally administered municipalities are defining the functions and powers for administrative departments at the provincial, municipal (prefectural), county, and township levels.

In addition to state appropriations, all local authorities are required to allocate a proper percentage of their reserve funds for educational purposes. Most of township revenues are supposed to be used for education. Local authorities may levy an extra tax for education, which is to be used exclusively to improve teaching facilities for elementary education. State-owned enterprises, public organizations, and individuals are being encouraged to run schools under the guidance of the local authorities, and other units are being encouraged to make donations to help develop education.

Vocational and Technical Education: restructuring secondary education and vigorously promoting vocational and technical education.

Vocational and technical education are the weakest link in the chain of China's education. All units engaged in highly specialized and technical work are now or soon will be required to employ graduates from vocational and technical schools ahead of those who have not received a qualification certificate.

Beginning at the middle-school level, schools are being divided into regular senior middle-schools and vocational and technical senior middle-schools. China hopes to have regular senior middle-school graduates enter regular colleges and universities and vocational/technical-school graduates receive advanced vocational and technical education. The current ratio of regular senior middle-schools to vocational and technical senior middle-schools is seven to three. By 1990, enrollment in vocational and technical senior middle-schools is targeted to equal that of regular senior middle-schools in most areas.

Although the current focus is on developing secondary vocational and technical education, with an emphasis on specialized secondary schools, advanced vocational and technical institutions also are developing the capacity to enroll graduates of secondary vocational and technical schools as well as employees experienced in special fields who have passed the entrance examinations.

To alleviate the serious shortage of teachers trained in vocational and technical education, units and departments that run vocational and technical schools are recruiting teachers from among their own personnel. Also, specialized technicians, master craftsmen, teachers, scientists, and engineers from other units are being asked to serve as part-time instructors, and vocational and technical normal schools and colleges will soon be established.

Enrollment: reforming enrollment planning of institutions of higher education and the system of job assignment on graduation and extending their decision-making power.

By the end of the twentieth century, China's goal is to have built a well-proportioned, rationally tiered system of higher education that embraces a complete range of disciplines and areas, with senior specialists trained basically at home, and institutions of higher education contributing substantially to China's independent scientific and technological development and solving major theoretical and practical problems that develop in the course of socialist modernization. To attain this goal, government control over institutions of higher education is being reduced. Under the guidance of the state's unified policies and plans in education, the decision-making power of colleges and universities is being extended; and their ties with production units, scientific research institutions, and similar sectors are being strengthened. Several specific reforms are therefore being implemented.

Unified enrollment of all students for colleges and universities in accordance with state plans and guaranteed job assignment for all graduates by the state are being replaced by three new methods. The first is enrollment according to state plans. These students are being enrolled according to the state's immediate and long-range requirements, and are being supported by the state. After graduation, they will be assigned jobs in line with state plans and in light of their own wishes, the recommendation of their schools, and the choice of units wishing to employ them. To ensure that a certain number of graduates go to work in outlying areas and in trades and professions where working conditions are harsh, a number of students, forming a fixed proportion in the state plan, are being enrolled from these areas, trades, and professions. Preferential treatment will be accorded to graduates who go to work in these areas. China also hopes to train a certain number of students for the People's Liberation Army to meet the needs of national defense.

Second is enrollment by commission from units that need graduates. Concerned units are paying training fees, as prescribed in contracts they have signed with schools, for students to enter institutions of higher education. After graduation, the students will be assigned to work in these units in accordance with the contract.

Third is enrollment of self-supporting students outside the state plan. These students are paying tuition for their training. After graduation, they may find jobs by themselves or be employed through their schools' recommendation.

Students in all three categories must pass the National College Entrance Examinations before they may be enrolled. Those in normal schools and/or those who will work in hardship after graduation will receive their board and lodging expenses from the state; their tuition and fees for extras will be waived. Scholarships are being granted to students with distinguished academic records, and subsidies are being given to those who are unable to support themselves. (Former regulations continue to be applied to students who already were enrolled in colleges and universities at the time the regulations went into effect.)

Decision-making power is being expanded for colleges and universities. Institutions of higher education now have the power to accept commissions for training students and enroll self-supporting students outside state plans; to redefine the goals of different specialities, draw up teaching plans and syllabuses, and compile and select teaching materials; to accept commissions from, or cooperate with, other units in scientific research and technological development and form associations for teaching, scientific research, and production; to appoint or remove vice presidents and other cadres at various levels; to decide how to use the funds allocated by the state for capital construction and other purposes; and to retain funds generated from educational and academic exchanges with other countries. In light of differing conditions in different colleges and universities, the state is endowing them with other powers. At the same time, the state and its departments in charge of education are strengthening overall guidance and control of higher education. A system is being introduced by which colleges and universities will be run by the three levels of the central authorities, the provinces (and the autonomous regions and centrally administered municipalities), and the key cities.

The readjustment and restructuring of higher education are to serve the needs of economic and social development and scientific and technological progress. The distribution of disciplines offered by institutions of higher education is being changed. Weak departments and specialities, such as finance and economics, political science and law, and management, are being improved, and new disciplines are being developed. The ratio of advanced professional schools to colleges is to be adjusted, with emphasis on the development of the former. To strengthen scientific research and produce competent specialists, postgraduate studies are being improved and a number of new, key disciplines in those colleges and universities that are best qualified according to peer review are being established. Overall, colleges and universities are increasing their academic potential through reform, expansion, and associations of all kinds, but generally no new institutions are being built.

Course content and teaching methods are being reformed, and teaching quality is being improved by integrating theory with practice. To eliminate existing defects in teaching methods, China is broadening the areas covered by different specialities; simplifying and updating course content; adding practice sessions; reducing the number of required courses and increasing electives; introducing a course-credit system and dual degrees; giving more time to students for individual study and extracurricular activities; and expanding the work-study program. To improve the quality of teaching and raise the academic level of teachers in colleges and universities, all professors and associate professors who have heavy teaching loads will now spend one year out of every five on advanced studies, scientific research, or academic exchanges. Teaching facilities are to be improved by increasing modern equipment and updating and replenishing laboratories and libraries.

Leadership: strengthening leadership and mobilizing all factors to ensure successful restructuring of education.

The State Education Commission, which replaced the Ministry of Education, was established to monitor the implementation of major principles and policies concerning education, make overall arrangements for the development of educational undertakings, coordinate educational work of various departments, and provide general plans and guidance for educational reform. Additionally, in keeping with other reforms to decentralize education, local authorities now have more power and bear greater responsibility for the development of education. Party committees and governments at all levels are asked to give strategic priority to education and to make its development one of their chief tasks and an essential factor in their appraisal of their subordinates' performance.

More initiative is being given to all quarters—most importantly, to the ten million teachers in China. Major reform measures concerning specific schools are not to be implemented without prior discussion by the teachers affected. A system of congresses of teachers and other employees, with teachers at the core, is to be established and strengthened to ensure more democratic management and supervision. Party organizations in schools are abandoning the practice of monopolizing management, and are instead concentrating on strengthening the party and improving its ideological and political work.

Exchanges with foreign countries are being increased through all possible channels, including the recently established Chinese Education Association for International Exchange, an offshoot of the State Education Commission's Bureau of Foreign Affairs.

While all the reforms in the Decision focus on restructuring school education, the central committee also has instructed the State Education Commission to initiate additional reforms to improve and strengthen adult education (involving cadres, workers and other employees, and peasants) and radio and television education. Thus, in June 1985, the State Education Commission announced the following priorities: implement the education reforms announced in May 1985; encourage legislation regarding elementary education and teacher training; assess the need for and impact of vocational education; streamline the administration of higher education institutions; and draft reforms for the adult education system.

The reforms that are being implemented during the period 1985–90 are intended to have major impact on China's educational system. However, some concerns about the proposed reforms have been expressed by persons knowledgeable about China. These include recognition that the pace of reforms in China often takes place more slowly than expected: in some cases, such as increasing teachers' salaries, delays could create political difficulties. Also, local bureaucrats have sometimes been obstacles to change, and they now have been delegated even more authority. In addition, some universities can be expected to focus more time and energy on generating new revenue rather than on creating high-quality programs. Competitive universities that have broader financial bases will best weather cuts in central government funding; lesser institutions may be unable to survive.

2
Recurring Themes

The evolution of China's education system evinces several recurring themes or characteristics. These include an emphasis on science and technology, sending students abroad for advanced training, national examinations, central control over and responsibility for all aspects of education, and features such as the relationship between education and personal advancement. Some of these themes, such as the role of schools in inculcating values, are common to virtually all eras and nations; others are almost unique. This chapter will examine themes that have had, and continue to have, special significance in China.

Emphasis on Scientific and Technical Subjects

For more than a century, leading Chinese officials have emphasized the relationship between science and engineering on the one hand and modernization and national security on the other. Defeats at the hands of "barbarians" with better technologies convinced such officials that China had to master the new technologies and scientific disciplines on which they were based in order to regain her rightful role in international affairs. Because China was starting from behind and faced increasingly dangerous adversaries with superior weapons and industrial equipment, she had to concentrate her resources in fields considered most critical to self-strengthening.

The lessons of the late nineteenth century were reinforced by the example of the Soviet Union. The Soviets had made dramatic progress since 1917. Part of the reason, in the view of Chinese leaders—and, between 1949 and 1960, their Russian advisers—was that Soviet schools emphasized technical training. During the 1950–66 period, nearly half of all Chinese college students were enrolled in science and engineering programs, and many, perhaps most, of the schools established during these years were technical institutes. One reason the PRC could devote so much attention to the sciences was that it had inherited a sizable corps of scientists and engineers. Similar capabilities, expectations, and objectives continue to shape China's educational policies and priorities. Conversely, one of the charges leveled at the "Gang of Four" is that it attempted—successfully—to weaken China by undermining the education system, especially the teaching of science and technology.

Sending Students Abroad

The Qing (Ch'ing) dynasty began to send students abroad in the 1870s for modern training even before abolishing the civil service examination and other keystones of the traditional system of education. However, both then and under subsequent regimes, including those of the Nationalists and the Communists, officials have been ambivalent about sending the cream of China's youth to study in foreign countries. While the advanced technical training and other skills acquired by exchange students are badly needed, and thus highly valued, certain "contaminating" ideas about politics, social organization, and other matters are less welcome.

Thousands of Chinese students studied abroad, many at the graduate level, in the decades between 1900 and 1950. In the years since, surviving members of this group of "returned students" have been alternately praised and excoriated. Presently, they again hold positions of prestige and responsibility; but many are too old to make major contributions. Lest one underestimate the importance of this group, or of foreign study in general, to China's modernization effort, it should be noted that virtually all senior officials of the Chinese Academy of Sciences have studied abroad.

During the 1950s and early 1960s, nearly 40,000 Chinese youth studied in the Soviet Union and Eastern Europe. They, too, have experienced severe political criticism (for having studied abroad, for being elitist or ivory-tower intellectuals, etc.), but are again playing key roles in the quest for rapid modernization. Their ranks are being augmented by the return of students and mid-career specialists sent abroad in the post-Mao period. Overseas study continues to provide opportunities for postgraduate training that cannot be obtained in China.

National Examinations

National college entrance examinations have played an important role in the PRC (except during the Cultural Revolution). Although the content of the examinations currently administered is vastly different than in traditional China, the tests are highly reminiscent of the old civil service examinations. Passing the examinations virtually assures one of a personally rewarding career; failure leaves few attractive

17

alternatives. Whether or not an individual succeeds often depends in part on location of residence and the opportunity to attend a good school. Having educated or politically connected parents also helps.

Examinations are administered nationally, but the results are evaluated on a province-by-province basis. Each province has a quota at the principal national institutions, and many provincial schools accept students only from within their boundaries.

Central Guidance and Control

Efforts to control schools throughout the country did not begin with the establishment of the PRC; more than four decades earlier, Chinese officials had determined that it was necessary and desirable to exercise such control. They were motivated in part by the realization that the legitimacy of the regime rested on its ability to strengthen the country and improve the life of the citizenry. To ensure that adequate numbers of educated people were available to fill new roles, the central government believed it prudent to oversee the school system. In other words, since officials would be held responsible for the performance of the schools, they wanted control over what happened in the classroom in order to ensure high quality. A second motivation throughout the twentieth century has been to inculcate values supportive of various political regimes and their objectives. The reforms being implemented since May 1985, while decentralizing authority somewhat, still leave responsibility for overall national policy and coordination of education in the hands of the central government's State Education Commission.

3

The Structure of China's Education System

Overall responsibility for all schools in China rests with the State Education Commission (SEDC—formerly the Ministry of Education), but only a small percentage of all schools are administered directly by the SEDC. Most are under the direct supervision of either provincial or municipal bureaus of education, or are run by such other local units as municipalities and counties. In addition, several other ministries, (e.g., Metallurgy, Energy, and Railways) administer secondary schools, colleges, and universities. Although the State Education Commission has overall responsibility for these schools, it is not involved in their day-to-day activities. Provincial-level bureaus of education and higher education share responsibility for schools located within their jurisdiction with the SEDC and/or other ministries. In some cases (e.g., supervision of provincial key schools), the local bureau has primary responsibility for matters such as budgetary allocations and placement of graduates.

Only a small percentage of schools are funded directly through the SEDC budget. Schools under the direct supervision of provincial authorities are supported by provincial budgets. A portion of their money for education comes to the province in the form of allocations from the national treasury; these allocations are designed to supplement local resources. The per capita amount channeled into provincial accounts reflects governmental efforts to redistribute funds to needy or high priority regions and activities. Thus, most village schools are funded from local revenues and tuition fees. One anomaly in present-day China is that peasants must pay a nominal fee (or an indirect tax) to support local schools while urban residents have access to free education.

China's education system consists of several types of units. Each is described briefly below.

Nurseries and Kindergartens

Strictly speaking, nurseries and childcare centers are not part of the formal education system. Found in many factories and communities, they are essentially daycare centers for the convenience of working parents. Kindergartens, on the other hand, are part of the education system, even though they do not engage in the same kind of academic instruction as do schools at other levels. Kindergarten education consists of games, sports, lessons, observation, handwork, and recreation. Typically, more attention is paid to games, observation, handwork, and daily activities than to lessons. In 1985, China had 172,300 kindergartens, with 549,500 teachers and a total enrollment of 14,796,900 children. The five types of kindergartens include those that are:

1. *Administered by provincial and municipal educational departments.* Teachers and administrative staff are appointed by educational departments, at different government levels, and funds come from the state educational department. These are the main kindergartens, some of which are model ones, particularly those administered by teacher-training institutions for purposes of experimentation with new methodologies.
2. *Administered by non-educational institutions or enterprises.* All teachers, administrative staff, and funds are provided by the institution or enterprise that runs the kindergarten.
3. *Administered by neighborhood committees.* Funds come from the neighborhood committee and from the parents' units or employers; some support also may come from local governments. Teachers and administrative staff are appointed by the kindergarten.
4. *Administered by villages.* Funds come from collective economic organizations. Teachers and administrative staff are appointed by village governments.
5. *Privately managed.* Expenses are provided mainly by the children's parents. Teachers and administrative staff are appointed by the kindergarten principal.

Kindergartens mainly are day schools, but there also are some boarding kindergartens. In rural areas, kindergartens or classes for preschool children are seasonal.

In October 1981, the then-Ministry of Education (now the State Education Commission) issued "A Program for Kindergarten Education (Draft)," which is the guide for preschool education at the present time. In light of the program, kindergartens teach subjects such as:

- *Hygiene.* This teaches children general knowledge about hygiene and cultivates good habits and abilities.

- *Sports.* This introduces children to physical exercise to ensure healthy growth and development, and stresses basic movement, such as coordination and good posture.
- *Ethics.* This cultivates moral character, civilized behavior, and respect for China, its people, physical labor, science, and public property.
- *Language.* This teaches children to speak clearly and correctly in *putonghua* or standard Chinese. It also enriches their vocabulary, develops their ability to think, teaches them to express themselves orally, and cultivates in them a preliminary interest in literature.
- *General Knowledge.* This widens children's field of vision, helping them enrich their basic knowledge of the social and natural environment. It cultivates in them an interest in understanding society and their natural environment and promotes a desire for knowledge. Gradually it assists them in acquiring a correct understanding of the people and things around them. It helps them develop their attention span, observation, memory, imagination, and verbal expression.
- *Arithmetic.* This helps children perform simple calculations, such as addition or subtraction from one to ten, and teaches elementary knowledge about geometric figures, time, and space. It cultivates an interest in calculation, helps develop the ability to think abstractly, and encourages accuracy, flexibility, and mental agility.
- *Music.* This teaches children elementary skills in music and dance, helps them develop rhythm, and cultivates an interest in music and dance.
- *Art.* This teaches children to observe shape, color, and structure. It also introduces them to drawing and handicrafts (clay toys, paper toys, etc.) as a means of self-expression. It cultivates in them an appreciation of art, nature, and society, and develops their observation, imagination, and creativity.

Kindergarten children are grouped according to age. Three- to four-year-olds belong to the lowest class; four- to five-year-olds to the middle class; and five- to six-year-olds to the highest class. Lowest class periods last 10 to 15 minutes (six periods in the morning, eight periods in the afternoon); middle class periods last 20 to 25 minutes (10 periods in the morning, 11 periods in the afternoon); highest class periods last 25 to 30 minutes (12 in the morning, 12 in the afternoon).

Even though approximately 14.8 million children attend kindergarten in China, given the size of this particular age cohort, it is readily apparent that only a relatively small percentage of all children attend kindergartens—not surprising, since most kindergartens are located in urban areas. Even though academic skills per se are not a part of the kindergarten program, children who attend such facilities—particularly the better kindergartens for which tuition is charged—have a clear advantage over those who first enter school at the age of six or seven.

Preschool teachers mainly are graduates of training schools for kindergarten teachers. In 1985, China had 57 such schools offering three- and four-year courses. In addition, there were 200 courses for kindergarten teachers offered by secondary normal schools and 300 courses offered by senior middle-schools and vocational middle-schools. The state and local education departments offered radio, television, and correspondence schools and night school courses and lectures to train and raise the level of kindergarten teachers. Specialized teachers graduated from preschool education departments of teachers' universities or colleges. At present, there are ten such specializations.

A primary education department under the State Education Commission is in charge of kindergarten education. There also are preschool education sections or offices under the education departments of provinces, municipalities, and autonomous regions and organizations of workers in the science of preschool education. The Chinese Central Research Institute of Educational Science has a section for research in preschool education, and in 1979 the Preschool Education Research Institute of China, a nongovernmental agency, was established for practical research and academic exchange.

Primary Schools

According to a pamphlet issued by the State Education Commission in 1986, the task of China's primary school education is to enable children to develop morally, intellectually, physically, and aesthetically and to establish the foundation for an educated and well-disciplined generation with lofty aspirations and excellent moral character. The training objectives of full-time primary schools are:

1. To inculcate in pupils a love for the country and the people and a strong interest in labor and science, and to foster good morals, strong will, and appropriate behavior.
2. To help students develop comprehension, expressivity, and calculating ability, grasp rudimentary knowledge about nature and human society, and acquire the ability to observe, think, and study independently.

3. To enable pupils to develop a healthy physique, good social habits, familiarity with manual labor, and the ability to take care of themselves.
4. To cultivate a love for beauty and the beginning of aesthetic judgment.

China has a vast territory with a huge population encompassing 56 nationality groups. Economic and cultural backgrounds and development vary in different areas because of natural conditions and historical reasons. Universalization of education in a country such as China inevitably assumes unique characteristics of its own. The key to universalizing primary education lies in the rural areas. At present, networks of primary school education have been established in many parts of rural China.

The coexistence of five-year and six-year primary schools suits the uneven development in different regions. Children begin school at the age of six or seven. In areas sparsely inhabited by national minorities, schooling is more flexible.

According to 1985 statistics, there were 832,300 primary schools throughout the country, with pupils totaling 133,701,800. The enrollment rate of school-age children had increased from 20 percent in 1949 to 95.9 percent in 1985. The percentage of girls enrolled in primary school also had increased substantially—from 28 percent of the total enrollment in 1951 to 43.8 percent of the total enrollment in 1984. The dropout rate from primary schools was reduced in 1985 to 3.3 percent. Officials are disturbed, however, by the apparent reversal of this trend. New economic opportunities, especially in the countryside, have enabled youth to take jobs, often at an early age, and this in turn has increased the dropout rate.

The state provides special support to areas inhabited by national minorities to develop education. According to 1984 statistics, minority-nationality pupils in China numbered 9,100,000—more than nine times the figure for 1951.

China is working toward a basic universalization of primary school education by 1990, with the exception of very sparsely populated areas and outlying regions inhabited by minority nationalities. As of October 1985, one-third or 731 of the counties in China had made primary education universal. The policy of universalizing education has led to three types of primary schools.

Full-time Primary Schools. These are the main body of primary school education. Their teaching plans, syllabuses, and materials are drafted by the State Education Commission, but the provinces, municipalities, and autonomous regions usually modify them to bring them into alignment with local conditions. Experimental primary schools and key schools are the mainstay of full-time schools.

Primary schools, like Chinese educational institutions at other levels, are of two general types, "key" and "ordinary." Key (or key-point) schools are given the best teachers, best equipment, and best students. Local offices or bureaus of education (at the district, municipal, or provincial level) designate and "assist" key schools. The ratio of key to ordinary schools varies from place to place. In general, the ratio is highest in large cities and lowest in the countryside. Indeed, there are few key schools in the countryside. Whether or not one is able to attend a key primary school is partly an accident of geography. If one happens to live in an area served by a key school, one might attend on the basis of a "neighborhood schools" principle. However, in at least some cases, students are selected for the upper primary grades on the basis of locally prepared competitive examinations. Successful candidates may cross district lines to attend key schools.

Rural Primary Schools. These offer only four subjects: Chinese, arithmetic, general knowledge, and ethics.

Simple Primary Schools. These include double-shift schools, mobile schools, classes, and groups where only Chinese and arithmetic are taught. Their teaching plans and materials are prepared by the provinces, municipalities, and autonomous regions.

Primary schools are administered mainly by local governments, but factories, mines, enterprises, and administrations in cities and neighborhood committees in the countryside are encouraged to manage their own schools. In addition, people in both urban and rural areas are allowed to raise funds and administer schools of their own.

According to 1985 statistics, China had 6,021,000 primary-school teaching and administrative staff, including 5,376,800 teachers, of which 2,093,600 were women. The ratio of teachers to pupils was 1 to 25. Many primary school teachers are trained in secondary normal schools, especially those who teach in large cities. These schools numbered 1,008 in 1984 throughout the country, with a student population of 511,000. Normal schools enrolling junior middle-school graduates have a three- or four-year school system, while those enrolling senior middle-school graduates are two-year schools. In 1984, 503,000 primary-school teachers studied in 1,782 schools of advanced studies for teachers.

Under teaching plans adopted by the State Education Commission in 1981 and 1984, 40 weeks every year, optimally, are devoted to teaching (including reviewing and examinations) and 12 weeks to winter and summer vacations (including vacations during busy farm-ing seasons for rural schools). The curriculum includes 11 subjects: politics, Chinese, arithmetic, natural science, foreign language (in schools where teachers are available), geography, history, physical education, music, fine arts, and manual labor. In every school year, six subjects run concurrently for lower grades, seven for the middle grade(s), and nine for higher grades. There are 24 or 25 class hours every week for lower grades, 26 for the middle grade, and 27 for higher grades. (In six-year schools, the per-week number of class periods is 23, 25, and 26 for lower, middle, and higher grades respectively.) In addition, there are five class-hours for extracurricular activities (six periods for six-year schools), of which two are for scientific and tech-nological or recreational activities, two for sports, and one for weekly meetings or Young Pioneer activities.

The principle guiding China's primary school education is to enable the children to develop politically, intellectually, physically, and aesthetically. The following points are stressed.

Strengthening education in patriotism and Communist ethics. A course in morals is offered, with a syllabus that stipulates the objective of the course is to cultivate the pupils' patriotism, collectivism, and sense of mastery over their own affairs. The pupils are taught to love the country, the people, labor, science, socialism, the collective, and public property; to study hard, and observe discipline; to be polite, honest, and modest; to be brave and lively; and to be diligent and frugal. The provinces, municipalities, and autonomous regions prepare their own teaching materials for the course in morality. History and geography courses also serve this purpose. Teaching syllabuses and materials are provided. For middle and higher grades there are lessons in manual labor. Many schools have their own bases for labor lessons. Some localities have their own teaching program for this subject. The State Education Commission issued Rules for Pupils as a guide for students' everyday conduct. Every school has Young Pioneer organizations with instructors, and their activities are included in the timetable. Educa-tional activities for each specific period of time are included in the work plans of the schools. In addition, all teachers are required to combine moral education with the imparting of knowledge.

Developing the pupils' abilities and enlightenment while enhancing their rudimentary knowledge of the Chinese language and arithmetic. Chinese lessons constitute 40.3 percent of the total class periods (39 percent in six-year schools). The pupils are required to master *Pinyin*, or the Chinese phonetic alphabet, and learn 3,000 Chinese characters. Arith-metic lessons account for 24.8 percent of the total class periods, giving the pupils an elementary knowledge of quantitative relations and spatial forms and enabling them to do fundamental operations with integers, decimals, and fractions correctly and speedily, think logically, and have some idea about space. They are expected to be able to solve simple, practical problems related to everyday life and labor. The course in natural science is a combination of rudimentary physics, chemistry, astronomy, geography, biology, and physiological hygienics. This course enables the children to know something about nature, and how man explores, utilizes, and protects it. It usually is offered to third graders and above, but can be opened to first and second graders where teachers are available.

Organizing extracurricular activities to enrich the children's cultural life. Various interest groups, performing groups, and sports teams are organized in the schools, and there are children's palaces (homes) and various after-school centers outside the schools. Recent statistics show that there are some 8,000 establishments for children to attend after school.

In summary, there is tremendous variation in primary schools in China, deriving to some extent from the uneven quality of teaching staffs. Many primary school teachers, especially in rural areas, have had less than the equivalent of a middle-school education. Often their sole qualification is that they were once students in the schools in which they now teach. The serious shortage of trained primary school teachers results in part from their low status and political vulnerability throughout much of the PRC's history. The teaching profession as a whole has had difficulty attracting qualified people, and the problem has been most severe at the beginning level of the system. The new reforms include measures to make the profession more attractive, but it will take time to overcome the stigma of the past.

Secondary Schools

Secondary education in China consists of junior (lower) secondary (middle) school or junior high school, which provides basic knowledge and forms part of the nine years of compulsory education, and senior (upper) secondary (middle) school, which includes regular senior high school, vocational school, technical school, normal school, and agricultural school. In 1985, there were 93,200 secondary schools, including 75,900 junior high schools and 17,300 comprehensive secondary schools and independent senior high schools. There were approximately 47,059,600 students studying at these schools—39,648,300 in junior secondary schools, 7,411,300 in senior secondary schools. According to a

State Education Commission publication, nearly 70 percent of primary-school graduates were admitted into junior high schools, 46 percent of junior-high-school graduates into senior high schools, and 31.5 percent of high-school graduates into schools of higher learning. During the past 36 years, China has trained more than 270 million secondary-school graduates.

As a result of China's effort to universalize education through junior secondary school, a more even distribution of middle schools throughout China is occurring. In large and medium-sized cities such as Beijing, Tianjin, and Shanghai, junior-high-school education has become common. Good secondary schools or senior secondary schools also are not uncommon in many counties. Junior secondary schools are in nearly every town. Educational advancements also have made progress in remote areas: in 1985, there were 55 secondary schools in Tibet, 2,100 in Xinjiang, 430 in Ningxia, and 410 in Qinghai; before 1949, there were only eight secondary schools in Xinjiang, five in Ningxia, four in Qinghai, and none in Tibet.

In order to meet the needs of China's developing economy and create jobs for secondary-school graduates, agricultural schools began being established in the late 1950s. Vocational-school education suffered greatly, however, from 1966 to 1976. In those years, secondary schools with radical "red-vs.-expert" curricula replaced intermediate vocational schools. The year 1978 marked the beginning of the restoration of vocational- and technical-school education. Some senior secondary schools were merged, others were converted into agricultural, vocational, or technical secondary schools. By 1985, 2,295,700 students were enrolled in 8,070 agricultural secondary schools and 1,869,300 students were enrolled in 7,057 vocational, technical, and specialized secondary schools—the combined total of 4,165,000 representing 36 percent of secondary-school students. While China currently is stressing the conversion of its regular secondary schools into specialized vocational and technical institutions, there is much popular resistance to this policy in rural areas, where parents prefer to expose their children to something other than agriculture. Progress is painfully slow. The 36 percent of China's secondary students enrolled in agricultural and vocational/technical schools in 1985 represented only a 6 percent increase from 1979; in 1988, the figure remains steady at 36 percent.

In 1985, China had 3,556,800 secondary-school teachers and administrative staff; of those, 2,651,600 worked at vocational schools.

Generally, both junior and senior secondary schools last three years, although a few secondary schools are experimenting with four years for junior and three years for senior students. Each school year is

40 weeks in duration, divided into two equal terms, with 10 to 12 weeks for vacation. There are six classes per day—30 or 31 classes per week for junior-secondary-school students, 26 to 29 classes per week for senior-secondary-school students.

The curriculum for junior and senior secondary schools, according to a pamphlet produced by the State Education Commission in 1986, includes the following:

Subject	Junior secondary school 1	2	3	Senior secondary school 1	2	3	Total class hours
Political and ideological education	2	2	2	2	2	2	384
Chinese language	6	6	6	5	4	4	1,000
Mathematics	5	6	6	5	5	5	1,026
Foreign language	5	5	5	5	5	4	932
Physics		2	3	4	3	4	500
Chemistry			3	3	3	3	372
History	3	2		3			266
Geography	3	2			2		234
Biology	2	2				2	192
Physiology and hygiene			2				64
Physical education	2	2	2	2	2	2	384
Music	1	1	1				100
Fine arts	1	1	1				100
Weekly required course hours	30	31	31	29	26	6	5,554
Elective course hours					4	24	240
Job training	2 weeks*			2 weeks*		2 weeks*	576

*Job training hour calculation is based on four classes daily for both junior and senior secondary schools.

To fully exploit available teaching facilities and develop students' interests and special skills, many schools offer elective courses such as computer science, map-making, electronics, basic astronomy, oceanography, elementary medical science, formal logic, history of literature, theory of literature and art, ancient Chinese language, and a secondary foreign language. A number of schools conduct after-class lectures on science and technology. Subjects include astronavigation, fiber optics, bioengineering, lasers, new materials, new energy sources, and ocean development, to name a few. Most secondary schools also have organized recreational activities for the study of science and technology, art, and sports.

Secondary-school education is administered at five different government levels: central, provincial, city (prefecture), county, and town. The State Education Commission is charged with the following responsibilities:

- implementation of the principles and policies for secondary-school education as set by the state;
- overall planning of long- and intermediate-term development of secondary-schools and coordination of yearly plans;
- overall allocation of teaching staff, funds, and materials and setting of guidelines for staff quotas and standards for school buildings, equipment, expenditures, etc.;
- determining the basic educational system, teaching plans, and guidelines, and organizing the compilation and screening of basic teaching materials and reference books;
- playing a consultative and supervisory role; and
- drafting laws on education.

Provincial, city (prefecture), county, and town governments are responsible for the planning and implementation of detailed principles and guidelines suitable for their areas. They also have the right to decide their own jurisdiction. Thus, the growth of secondary-school education largely depends on the administration of county and city governments.

The sections of the Communist Party Central Committee's Decision on Reform of the Educational System that are particularly applicable to secondary-school education are as follows:

- The introduction of nine-year compulsory education will be conducted in a planned manner. The new schooling system will be instituted in cities comprising one-quarter of the nation's total population, in more affluent areas of coastal provinces, and in a small number of developed inland areas, before 1990. To achieve this goal, existing junior high schools are being expanded and new ones are being built.
- Efforts are underway to develop vocational and technical schools, replacing a number of senior high schools and/or incorporating vocational classes into normal secondary schools. By 1990, an equal number of students should be studying at senior high schools and vocational schools in most parts of the country.
- Further reform of secondary-school education will result in the establishment of principles for teaching materials and methods, management, and teaching plans and guidelines, as well as the compilation and editing of textbooks and improvement of teaching quality. According to the State Education Commission, these goals are conso-

nant with the principle of "gearing education to the modernization drive, world development, and the future."

Higher Education

The system of higher education is described in greater detail elsewhere in this *Introduction*. Briefly, in 1987 China had 1,063 institutions of higher education, of which 941 were colleges, universities, and professional training schools and 122 were short-term advanced vocational schools.

Detailed statistics available on enrollments in 1985 show there were 1,016 institutions of higher education in China, to which 619,200 students were admitted to degree programs—an increase of 30.3 percent over 1984. Of these, 317,900 entered undergraduate programs and 301,300 began special courses (courses designed for specific purposes); 435,500 of these students (both undergraduates and students in special courses) were enrolled as regular college students; 60,400 were sponsored by various organizations for training in colleges; 79,100 were in special training courses for cadres; 11,400 were in undergraduate or special courses for teachers; and 32,800 were day students who are not assigned jobs by colleges after graduation. This entering class brought the total number of students studying at the undergraduate level to 1,703,100—a 22 percent increase over 1984. In addition, in 1987, China had 1.8 million students enrolled in a variety of other forms of postsecondary education, most notably the Chinese Television University and numerous adult education courses.

Also in 1985, 46,500 students were admitted to graduate programs in universities, colleges, and research institutions, which doubles the number that were admitted to similar programs in 1984. This brought the total number of students working for master's or doctoral degrees to 87,200, a 51.4 percent increase over 1984.

In 1985, there were 5,000 full professors at Chinese institutions of higher education; the State Education Commission plans to increase this number to 30,000 by 1990. There also were 30,000 associate professors in 1985, 90 percent of whom were less than 55 years old; according to current plans, this number will increase to 120,000 by 1990.

Universities gear enrollments and job assignments to China's goals for economic construction and social development and its need for personnel with advanced professional skills. The emphasis remains to provide trained personnel to promote the development of the four modernizations—agriculture, defense, industry, and science and technology—but the area of science and technology has been broadened to include finance, management, and law.

Colleges and universities are administered by several different agencies, but all fall under the jurisdiction of the State Education Commission (SEDC). There are 37 institutions that are directly administered by the SEDC and its subordinate bureaus; 304 colleges are supervised and partially funded by several national ministry-level agencies (e.g., the Chinese Academy of Sciences, the Chinese Academy of Social Sciences, and the Ministry of Energy). The majority are administered by provincial and municipal bureaus of higher education. There are both key and ordinary schools, as well as regular and spare-time or continuing-education programs. Key institutions have the best faculties and facilities, enroll the most qualified students, and receive special support and financing. Chinese government authorities indicated in 1986 that the use of the "key" designation was to be eliminated; it appears that this term is rarely used now by the SEDC, but that it continues to be used by institutions that were granted this distinction in the past.

Education for Ethnic Minorities

In addition to the populous Han nationality, China has 55 minority nationalities. According to the national census in 1983, ethnic-minority people number 67,233,254, or 6.7 percent of the country's total population. The minority peoples are distributed over vast regions, most of them inhabiting remote areas far from cities. According to state law, in areas where ethnic minorities live in compact communities, autonomous regions, prefectures, and counties, nationality townships are established to develop the economy and culture in light of particular cultural characteristics.

Since the founding of the People's Republic of China, the government has instituted a series of policies to advance the education of minorities. The 1984 figures for ethnic-minority students in schools of various types at all levels were as follows: 9,100,611 in primary schools, 2,082,455 in regular and agricultural secondary schools, 94,474 in specialized and normal secondary schools, 69,333 in higher-education institutions. Regular preschool education has begun to show some progress in national minority areas. There are independent kindergartens and kindergarten classes attached to primary schools that teach in the language of the particular nationality.

Various types of primary and secondary schools have been established in minority areas to adapt to the different situations that exist. There are special schools in which teachers of ethnic minorities teach in their own languages. In areas where the people lead a nomadic life and live in scattered communities, boarding schools subsidized by the state have come into existence. Students receive stipends to attend these schools. In addition to teachers, the boarding schools are staffed with nurses who look after the students' daily life, hygiene, nursing, sewing, laundry, and extracurricular activities. In essence, teachers and nurses in these schools perform to a great extent the duties of family education. In mountainous areas, where the minority people live far apart, communications are poor, and education is backward, a certain number of boarding primary and secondary schools have been established to offer the children there more educational opportunities. In some pastoral areas, in addition to the boarding primary schools, there are teaching centers that combine concentrated teaching and scattered teaching, depending on the season. The principal subjects taught include the Han Chinese language (Mandarin), arithmetic, and general knowledge. In semi-hilly areas and on plains, where minority people live in permanent residences in compact communities, nonresident primary and secondary schools have been established.

The various minorities speak different languages and use different scripts. Some have adopted the spoken and written language of the Han majority. All retain their own spoken and written languages. A small number of ethnic minorities still have only an oral language and no written script. The government has helped these groups create written languages, but they have not yet been put into general use. In China, the spoken and written Han language is indispensible for communicating among various nationalities.

Thus, two principles are followed regarding the language to be used in teaching. First, it should accord with the governmental policy of national equality. Second, it should further the economic, scientific, and cultural progress of the various nationalities. As a result, minority-nationality primary and secondary schools follow several paths. The minority's oral and written language is used for teaching, while at the same time students learn the Han language. In other schools, lessons are taught in the Han language, but classes in the minority language also are provided. In schools for minorities that have only a spoken language and no written form, the minority language is used to aid teaching during the primary-school period; in the meantime, students are required to learn the Han language. During the secondary-school phase, teaching is supposed to be conducted entirely in the Han language.

In lesson content, attention has been paid to promoting the cultural traditions of the various minority peoples. Outstanding literary works and historical stories are included in minority-language lessons. Music, art, and sports focus on popular national traditions and characteristics. Minority history and local geography also are taught.

In minority-area schools, students are educated at every level to foster unity among the various nationalities.

Today, textbooks for primary and secondary schools in 17 minority languages are being compiled, translated, and published throughout China. Special publishing houses established in appropriate provinces and autonomous regions are producing 900 varieties of textbooks, totaling 21 million volumes, every year.

Specialized secondary education for ethnic minority groups includes technical secondary schools and teacher-training, or normal, schools. The five autonomous regions of Inner Mongolia, Xinjiang, Ningxia, Tibet, and Guangxi alone have 335 such schools. Technical or vocational secondary schools offer the following specialities: agriculture, animal husbandry, veterinary science, forestry, commerce, medicine and health, finance and banking, arts, and sports. Some specialities, such as the arts, have distinctive national characteristics. Talented minority people are trained in minority music, dance, fine arts, and musical instruments.

The Chinese government also has realized the importance of providing higher education to outstanding minority youths and training them for professions in areas of national needs. Minority youths receive higher education in several types of institutions.

There are 17 institutions for nationalities that enroll mainly minority students (95 percent of the student body). All these institutions conduct a regular four-year college course. They also have classes for training managerial personnel engaged in administration, economy, and education, and a preparatory course for entering college.

Autonomous regions and prefectures have established 79 higher-education institutions of various types. In addition, more than 60 institutions of higher learning in the hinterlands have established classes designed to meet the needs of minority areas. Students are recruited from ethnic minorities and assigned work in their home regions upon graduation.

Other colleges and universities throughout China also are open to minority people. In order to give minority students an even opportunity to receive higher education and to accelerate the training of qualified people needed in minority areas, the government has given preferential treatment to minority students in the annual entrance examination for colleges and universities. Admission scores are lowered for students from minority areas, and on the occasion of identical scores, minority applicants are given preference over Han applicants. Graduates of secondary schools where lessons are taught in a minority language are allowed to write the entrance exams in their own language. This enables thousands of minority youths to be admitted into higher-education institutions each year.

In addition to regular funds allocated by the state, national minority areas receive various kinds of subsidies from the state each year, some of which are spent to develop education. The state also appropriates a special fund of 150 million yuan each year to subsidize primary-school education in old revolutionary base-areas, minority areas, remote mountainous regions, and poverty-stricken districts.

The State Education Commission has a nationality-education department in charge of education for minority people. Provinces with greater populations of national minorities maintain a nationality-education office under the provincial education department or education commission or appoint a person to be in charge of nationality education. Departments below the provincial level also have a nationality-education section or a person in charge of nationality education.

Education for the Handicapped

In 1951, the Administration Council of the Central People's Government decreed in a "Decision on Reform of the Educational System" that governments at all levels should set up educational establishments for the handicapped, including the blind, deaf-mute, mute, and other physically disabled children, youth, and adults. By 1985, China had 375 schools teaching 41,700 blind, deaf-mute, and retarded students, so that some children who are handicapped physically, mentally, or emotionally were able to be admitted into primary and secondary schools close to their homes.

The schooling provided for handicapped children varies. For the blind, five or six years of primary school and three years of junior high school may be offered; for the deaf and mute, eight years of primary education and three years of junior high school are sometimes possible. For the retarded, there is no definite school period because the program still is experimental, although some schools are following an eight-year system.

According to the decree, the curriculum is designed to train students politically, intellectually, and physically. It includes courses in politics, Chinese language, mathematics, social and natural sciences, fine arts, rhythm, sports, and work skills. However, different schools have different emphases to suit their special needs. For example, schools for the blind put special emphasis on music and on skill-training to sharpen the students' sense of touch. They also devote more time to sports in order to develop students' physical strength and agility. Schools for deaf-mutes pay particular attention to vocal training to enhance the students' ability to speak and read lips. They also stress exercise and sports to develop the students' coordination and physical strength. Classes for the mentally retarded concentrate on music, sports, and games. Skill-training classes have been designed for senior primary-school students in all special schools to ensure adequate preparation for further professional training and entrance into society. Special textbooks and teaching materials for the study of language, math, sports, rhythm, etc., have been compiled and published to meet the needs of blind, deaf, and mute students.

Approximately 6,014 teachers are engaged in special education throughout China. The State Education Commission has opened a normal school in Nanjing to train special-school teachers of all types for assignments in different parts of the country and to give mid-career training to those already at work. Similar schools and training classes have been conducted by local governments to meet their own needs.

Although special education has made some progress, it still fails to meet actual needs. Governments at various levels are working on plans to further develop special education in order to provide handicapped children with a proper education.

Adult Education

When the People's Republic of China was founded in 1949, over 80 percent of the population was illiterate and only 20 percent of school-age children attended school. Therefore, the government stressed the development of education—adult education as well as full-time general education. The system of adult education combines traditional school education with specialized education, ranging from elementary to higher education, and includes adult schools, training centers, education classes, and other courses in various forms sponsored by government departments, democratic parties, factories, mines, industrial enterprises, academic institutions, and public organizations.

Since 1949, more than 150 million adults have learned to read and write. More than 39 million of these individuals have proceeded to reach the level of primary-school graduates. More than 12 million have qualified as graduates of secondary schools or technical schools, and more than two million have qualified as graduates of vocational colleges or universities. Between 1981 and 1985, 39,000 adults completed postgraduate studies, 1,535,000 graduated from regular colleges and universities, and more than 900,000 graduated from adult universities and colleges. In 1985, 3.5 million adults learned to read and write, more than eight million adults received primary education, and more than five million adults received regular secondary education. There were 4,189 specialized adult secondary schools with a total enrollment of

1,347,500 students, 689,800 of whom enrolled in 1985. In higher education, 1,216 institutions of adult education and 591 regular colleges and universities that conducted correspondence and night schools enrolled 787,800 adults (62,000 undergraduates and 725,800 in special courses), bringing the total adult enrollment to 1,725,100—208,500 undergraduates and 1,516,600 in special courses. In addition, adult schools of different levels and types conducted many continuing education courses, short-term courses, and supplementary classes of less than one year's duration.

Adult education is provided for peasants, workers and staff members, and cadres. For peasants, it is designed to provide study in political science, culture, and science and technology and training in work ethics. In China, 80 percent of the population lives in rural areas. The 1982 national census indicated that 80 million people aged 14 to 40 were illiterate or semi-illiterate; most of these individuals live in rural areas. The Chinese government hopes essentially to eliminate illiteracy by 1995. In rural areas, peasants learn to read and write in classes, small groups, or individually.

While the elimination of illiteracy is under way, efforts are being made to establish primary, secondary, and specialized and technical secondary schools for peasants. Of the more than 400 million peasants between the ages of 14 and 40, over 120 million are graduates of junior and secondary schools. Adult primary-school students study for two or three years in their spare time to attain the level of primary-school graduates. The curriculum usually includes language, arithmetic, and agriculture. Secondary schools are vocational in nature. In addition to language and mathematics, students study one or two elective subjects related to production, such as botany, zoology, physics, or chemistry.

Peasant technical secondary education is designed mainly for technicians and managerial personnel in rural areas and young peasants who are graduates of junior secondary schools. Technical schools administered by counties are an important form of technical education for peasants. In 1980, they were designated as specialized agricultural secondary schools focusing on farming, animal husbandry, sideline production, fisheries, industry, etc. It is their task to provide secondary-level education in agricultural science and technology to personnel who will work in rural areas. Study is for two or three years. Funds for peasant education are collected mainly from Chinese citizens, with appropriate subsidies provided by the government.

Workers' primary education is similar to that of regular primary schools, and is conducted in schools or study classes. Workers' secondary education is undertaken mainly in workers' secondary schools and workers' schools. Workers younger than 40 who have not attained the level of junior secondary-school graduates in language, mathematics, physics, and chemistry are given supplementary remedial courses. Workers who have less than third-grade skill-levels who have not received specialized technical training are provided with supplementary lessons in technical theory and on-the-job training. Workers and staff members who have graduated from junior secondary-schools or whose level is approximately that of junior secondary-school graduates attend secondary schools for systematic and regular specialized education. The schooling generally lasts three years for those released from work; those who receive education in their spare time are given an equivalent amount of training over an extended period of time.

Workers' regular and spare-time universities are the principal forms of higher education for workers and staff members. Their objective is to provide an education in basic theory and specialized knowledge that is on a par with that of graduates from institutions of higher education. Schooling generally lasts three years on a work-release basis, four years for spare-time education. Workers and staff members who have more than two years' work experience and have attained the level of senior secondary-school graduates are eligible. Generally, the course work relates to the students' employment. In 1986, a unified entrance examination (not the National College Entrance Examination) was instituted to select candidates for workers' universities. Applicants are assessed politically, intellectually, and physically; only the best are admitted.

Workers' specialized secondary schools and regular and spare-time universities are administered by factories, mines, enterprises, institutions, administrative or education departments of the government, and trade unions. Upon completing all required courses and passing prescribed examinations, workers are given graduation certificates. Their school record is recognized by the state. Upon graduation, they return to their former units or are assigned new jobs according to a prescribed plan.

Enterprises and corporations with unified accounting may allot no more than 1.5 percent of total wages for education funds, calculated as part of the costs of production. Administrative and other institutions may allot no more than 1.5 percent of the standard wages for the same purpose, calculated as part of the administrative and operational expenditures.

Cadre education is designed for those who serve as functionaries of state bureaus at various levels. The basic objective is to improve their command of Marxist theory, their specialized knowledge, and their scientific and cultural level, and to enhance their management capabilities. Regular education for cadres is in two tiers, secondary education and higher education.

Cultural secondary education for cadres corresponds to regular junior or senior secondary schools. Classes are conducted by party or cadre schools; workers' schools administered by factories or mines also accept cadres.

Specialized secondary schools or classes are for young or middle-aged cadres who have attained the cultural level of junior secondary-school graduates. Work-released schooling lasts two years. The curriculum provided is designed to meet the needs of the unit that administers the school. Teaching programs are based on the curricula of specialized secondary schools, with special characteristics of education for cadres added. Regular specialized secondary schools and workers' specialized secondary schools also conduct classes for cadres.

Administrative colleges are the principal form of higher education for cadres. Cadres are trained as senior managerial personnel for governments, enterprises, and institutions. Work-released schooling lasts two or three years. Subjects taught are similar to those required by regular higher-education institutions for the basic training of specialized personnel. In 1984, a total of 54 colleges for managerial cadres, all with independent organizational systems, had been established in various parts of China. Students totalled 15,103, and the number of graduates reached 817.

During the past five years, adult education in China has made significant progress. In the early days of the People's Republic of China, literacy classes and primary education were the major forms of adult education. Now, secondary and higher specialized education receive primary emphasis. Radio, television, and other non-traditional means of education are in wide use. To encourage people to improve their capabilities through self-study, a system of examinations for those who follow a self-study program has been instituted (see Chapter 6). Correspondence and evening education programs, conducted mainly by regular institutions of higher learning, are an important form of higher education for adults. Classroom teaching in evening universities is undertaken in their spare time by teachers from institutions of higher learning. Correspondence students study under the written guidance of teachers and receive personal guidance from the teachers at specified times. Correspondence education was instituted as an economical method of improving the theoretical, cultural, and vocational levels of workers and office personnel and training specialists. Many adults have been trained through correspondence courses over the past 30 years (there were 264,527 such students in 1983), and a large number have become specialists who are the mainstay of production, scientific research, management, and teaching.

Technical Education for Staff and Workers

Specialized, technical, and vocational secondary schools are available to assist staff and workers in China in obtaining additional education in their chosen field. Specialized secondary schools are designed to train middle-level professionals; students are required to master basic theories, specialized knowledge, and practical techniques in their fields. Technical schools provide middle-level skilled workers with basic knowledge of modern production techniques related to their specialities; students are required to be competent in fairly complicated work, observe rules, and carry out sophisticated production. Vocational schools, including agricultural schools, train middle- and primary-level technical and managerial personnel as well as reserve labor forces who have acquired certain specialized knowledge, technical theory, and production skills.

Specialized Secondary Schools. Specialized secondary education is an important component of China's vocational education system. In 1984, China had 2,293 specialized schools (excluding normal schools), including 697 for engineering, 367 for agriculture, 39 for forestry, 506 for medicine and pharmaceutics, 393 for finance and economics, 108 for politics and law, 37 for sports, 99 for the arts, and 47 for other specialities. Total enrollment was 811,100. In 1984, specialized secondary schools graduated 237,700 students and enrolled 350,900 new students. Specialized secondary schools are administered either by ministries and commissions under the State Council or by local authorities.

Teaching materials, including those for general courses and basic engineering courses, are compiled under the sponsorship of the State Education Commission. Materials for some basic technical courses and all specialized courses are compiled by the departments concerned. In 1984, more than 500 types of syllabuses and teaching materials were published.

There are eight branches of academic study in specialized secondary schools: engineering, agriculture, forestry, medicine, finance, politics and law, sports, and the arts. The total number of specialities exceeds 400. Schools offer courses in Marxist-Leninist theory, general knowledge, basic technology, and specializations. Approximately 75 percent of the total teaching time is devoted to the first three categories. Students majoring in engineering, agriculture, forestry, and medicine take a total of 20 courses. The ratio of theoretical courses to laboratory courses is seven to three for engineering, agriculture, forestry, and medicine, and eight to two for finance and politics and law.

Each year, students have vacations of at least two months.

Engineering schools have laboratory workshops, and agricultural schools have farms. The students not only work in the workshops or on the farms, but also learn skills in factories, in the countryside, and in hospitals. Teachers for these schools are expected to be college or university graduates. The current number of teachers is 118,500. After completing all the courses required by the teaching programs, including fieldwork and a graduation project, and passing the examinations, students are qualified to receive diplomas. There is a system of grants-in-aid in specialized secondary schools, with approximately 75 percent of the students receiving stipends. Majors in coal mining, the arts, sports, and nursing all receive grants. The government assigns students to jobs after graduation. Since 1949, China's specialized secondary schools have graduated a total of four million students.

Technical Schools. Technical schools have developed along with the growth of China's national economy. They are the major channel for training middle-level skilled workers. Such schools are sponsored by various departments in different areas of the country. In 1984, there were 3,465 technical schools, with a total enrollment of 639,000.

Technical schools enroll junior- and senior-high-school graduates. The length of schooling is three years for junior-high-school graduates and two years for senior-high-school graduates. In recent years, many schools also have begun to offer various training courses in rotation for workers in enterprises. Since 1949, technical schools have trained 2.4 million skilled workers for various sectors of the national economy.

Technical schools offer more than 400 specialities, including light and textile industries, coal mining, power generation, oil, machine building, electronics, chemical industry, metallurgy, geology, building materials, construction engineering, railway and highway construction, water transportation, post and telecommunications, civil aviation, commerce, and catering and service trades. Courses offered include Marxist-Leninist theory, general knowledge, technical theory, production practice, and physical education. Total teaching time is evenly divided between production practice and the study of general knowledge and technical theory. Production practice is conducted either in affiliated workshops or in factories related to the respective specialities. Students receive diplomas after completing all required courses and passing examinations. Technical schools are tuition-free and all students receive grants-in-aid.

In order to train new teachers and improve the teaching proficiency of in-service teachers, the state has established vocational and technical teachers colleges and teachers training schools. The technical schools themselves assist their faculty in increasing professional competence by organizing demonstration lectures, conducting short-term training courses, sponsoring study tours of factories, and encouraging self-study. The technical schools also organize research activities to improve teaching skills. Today, most provinces, municipalities, and autonomous regions have technical-school teaching institutes.

In 1984, the nation's technical schools employed 181,000 teachers and staff members, of whom 70,000 were teachers. Teaching materials for courses of general knowledge and basic technical theory are compiled by labor and personnel departments; those for specialized courses are prepared by various industrial departments. To date, more than 200 types of teaching materials have been published or are being compiled. China's technical schools are administered by the ministries and commissions concerned under the State Council, local industrial authorities, and industrial enterprises. Local labor and personnel departments at various levels also have their own technical schools, which generally are administered by their sponsors. Schools administered by central and local industrial authorities and labor and personnel departments are financed by central and local governments. Those administered by industrial enterprises are financed by the enterprises themselves.

Vocational Schools. China's vocational schools include vocational, agricultural, and professional secondary schools. In October 1980, the State Council approved a report on reforming the structure of high school education. The report, jointly drafted by the then Ministry of Education (now the State Education Commission) and the State General Bureau of Labor, indicated that the restructuring of China's high school education should focus on reform of senior-high-school education. It proposed a new policy of simultaneously developing general education and vocational and technical education, increasing full-time schools, work-study schools, and spare-time schools, and administering schools through various channels. By 1984, the number of vocational schools had risen to 7,002 (2,380 in urban areas and 4,622 in rural areas) with a total enrollment of 1,744,800 (837,700 in urban areas and 907,100 in rural areas).

Since 1980, several new forms of school admnistration have been created. Local education departments have either transformed some senior high schools into vocational and agricultural secondary schools or added vocational and agricultural classes to senior high schools. Classes are administered by education departments. Education departments, enterprises, and government institutions now jointly administer schools and industrial enterprises administer their own schools. Counties administer agro-technical secondary schools or agro-technical schools, and townships administer agricultural secondary schools. Finally, workers' technical education centers have been established. Vocational schools enroll junior-high-school graduates for schooling of two to three years. Some agricultural junior-secondary schools enroll primary-school graduates for schooling of three to four years.

According to 1982 statistics for 18 provinces, autonomous regions, and municipalities, 385 specialities were offered. Among them, 218 were related to engineering, 48 to agriculture and forestry, 20 to medicine, 40 to finance and trade, and 59 to politics and law, sports, culture, education, arts and crafts, and tourist services. The largest specialities were agronomy, agricultural electrification, farm machinery, accounting, statistics, finance and trade, tailoring, nursery training, cotton textile, building, chemical engineering, electrical engineering, electronics technology, machine processing, and manufacturing and benchwork.

Vocational and agricultural secondary schools offer four categories of courses: Marxist-Leninist theory, general knowledge, specialized courses, and production practice. Generally, 40 to 50 percent of teaching time is devoted to the first two, 50 to 60 percent to the last two.

In 1984, China had 103,800 full-time agricultural and vocational school teachers. They were drawn from university and college graduates, high-school teachers who were transferred to vocational or agricultural schools to teach specialized courses after receiving advanced study at colleges or specialized secondary schools, and engineers, technicians, and qualified skilled workers.

Vocational school graduates receive diplomas after passing academic and technical examinations. Some may be employed by industrial enterprises and government institutions; others may work for themselves or go on to further study.

Planned Reforms

Education in the People's Republic of China is, to say the least, an extremely large-scale enterprise. With over one million schools and more than 200 million students, the tasks of administration are enormous. Ultimate responsibility resides in the State Education Commission. However, in May 1985, the Central Committee of the Communist Party of China issued a "Decision on the Reform of the Educational Structure," and in April 1986, the Fourth Plenary Session of the Sixth National People's Congress approved the Seventh Five-Year Plan (1986–90) for National Economic and Social Development. Both will have major impacts on the educational system that has evolved over the past several decades. Changes planned include the following:

- Responsibility for elementary education is being transferred to local authorities and nine-year compulsory education is being instituted.
- The structure of secondary education is being readjusted, so that while education in regular senior middle-schools continues to be improved, greater efforts are being made to develop vocational and technical education. By 1990, it is anticipated that an equal number of students will be studying at regular senior middle-schools and vocational schools in most parts of the country.
- The enrollment planning of institutions of higher education and the system of job assignment upon graduation are being reformed. The decision-making power of individual institutions of higher education is being extended. Further efforts are being made to readjust the structure of the proportions and levels of specialities in higher education, improve the conditions of existing schools, and raise the overall quality of higher education. By 1990, it is planned that regular institutions of higher learning will enroll 750,000 full-time regular and professional undergraduate students and will recruit 55,000 graduate students. It is anticipated that, between 1986 and 1990, 2.6 million undergraduates and 180,000 graduate students will graduate from colleges and universities.
- Additional emphasis is being placed on adult secondary vocational and technical education and on adult higher-education, which will combine study with practical application. It is anticipated that between 1986 and 1990, adult higher-education institutions will train 2.1 million people to attain professional college-graduate level or above.
- Administration of educational institutions is being streamlined and decision-making power is being decentralized to relax state control over schools. Administration of institutions of higher education gradually will become the responsibility of major cities. Between 1986 and 1990, the state plans to increase the level of investment in education so that a total of 116.6 billion yuan will be allocated to education, a 72 percent increase over the amount spent in the Sixth Five-Year Plan (1981–85).

Essentially, the leadership of educational institutions is being strengthened to ensure a successful restructuring of the educational system. The development of science and education is a key national strategy. Education is viewed as a primary agent for early realization of the "four modernizations" of agriculture, industry, national defense, and science and technology. The study of scientific and technical subjects is regarded as especially critical in this regard, but the area of science and technology has been broadened to include the topics of finance, management, and law.

4

The State Education Commission and Higher Education in China

Higher education in the People's Republic of China is both a paradox and a puzzlement. Traditional and ideological predispositions toward orderliness and central control are reflected in a system that subordinates all colleges and universities, directly or indirectly, to a single State Education Commission. Yet this system is at the same time polycentric, diversified, and divided into several very different subsystems.

Prior to the Cultural Revolution, China had both a Ministry of Education, responsible for primary and secondary schools, and a separate Ministry of Higher Education. When the state bureaucracy was restored in the early 1970s, the responsibilities and personnel of the two former educational ministries were merged to form a new Ministry of Education (MOE). The duties of the Ministry of Education were much broader than those of the U.S. Department of Education. The MOE was responsible for both long- and short-range planning in education, including the construction and equipping of new facilities, determination of the number of students to be trained in various specialities, and the training and assignment of teachers and administrators. It also approved national and local budgets for education, set curricular requirements, and prepared standardized teaching materials for all levels and units in the education system.

However, in June 1985 the State Council decided that a mechanism was needed to provide the overall planning of the nation's education, a task beyond the scope of the Ministry of Education. Therefore, at the eleventh session of the Sixth National People's Congress Standing Committee, the Ministry of Education was disbanded and a State Education Commission was established. The position of the minister in charge of the commission is concurrently held by a vice premier of the State Council, who has eight full-time deputies. Many of the members of the commission are concurrently vice ministers or deputy chiefs of the State Planning Commission, the State Economic Commission, the State Science and Technology Commission, the Ministry of Finance, and the Ministry of Labor and Personnel.

The responsibility and decision-making powers of the State Education Commission (SEDC) are broader and more pervasive than those of the Ministry of Education. The SEDC determines the strategies, policies, and overall planning of the development program of China's education system and is responsible for the organization and coordination of efforts to promote and administer educational reforms. Provinces, autonomous regions, and municipalities directly under the administration of the central government decide independently whether they should establish local education commissions. According to government statistics, by the end of July 1986 nine provinces had established their own education commissions.

Many of the specific roles of the State Education Commission are described elsewhere in this publication. When it was established in June 1985, the SEDC announced the following priorities: to implement the education reforms announced in May 1985; to encourage legislation regarding elementary education and teacher training; to assess the need for and impact of vocational education; to streamline the administration of higher education institutions; and to draft reforms for the adult education system. While some progress has been made in these areas, a number of difficulties must still be overcome.

In addition to the State Education Commission, there are other important organizations and activities that have a role in higher education in China. These include the following.

Provincial Bureaus of Higher Education and Province-Run Schools

Provincial bureaus of higher education are responsible for one or more "provincial key" schools and a larger number of "ordinary" institutions. At present, provincial key institutions generally are less impressive and less prestigious than are national key schools. They also are funded at a significantly lower level. Students in provincially run colleges are drawn almost exclusively from that province. When they graduate, students from provincial colleges normally are assigned to jobs within the province, but there are exceptions. In most cases, the student affairs division of the provincial bureau of higher education shares responsibility for the placement of those graduating from province-run schools with the provincial labor bureau and the provincial office of the State Planning Commission. In some cases, the college itself also plays a role in placement decisions.

Institutions Administered by Other Ministry-Level Agencies

Some colleges in this category are supervised jointly by the ministry-level agency and the State Education Commission (e.g., Zhejiang University is under the "dual authority" of the Chinese Academy of Sciences and the State Education Commission); others are run jointly by the ministry-level agency and a provincial bureau of higher education (e.g., most agricultural colleges and technical schools). Colleges administered in part by other ministry-level agencies range from medical schools (Ministry of Public Health) to music conservatories (Ministry of Culture). Other examples include the East China Petroleum Institute (Ministry of Energy), Harbin College of Shipbuilding (State Shipbuilding Corporation), and the Graduate School of the Chinese Academy of Social Sciences. The principal mission of these schools is to train professionals for careers in fields directly related to the functional responsibilities of the parent ministry or academy. Graduates normally are assigned to positions in enterprises or research institutes subordinate to the parent agency. Placement is the responsibility of the supervising agency (in conjunction with other relevant organizations).

Although funds for academic and administrative expenses (e.g., salaries, student support, and libraries) of institutions run by ministry-level agencies are provided through the SEDC, supplemental funding, primarily for equipment and research, is provided by the parent agency. Though usually tied to specific research projects, such funding provides a very important addition to the university's budget and, to the extent that students participate in research projects, directly augments the academic and administrative allocation from the SEDC.

Chinese Communist Party Schools

One category of schools that apparently does not fall under the jurisdiction of the SEDC should be mentioned, since at least some instruction is at the postsecondary level: the schools run by the Chinese Communist Party. Courses include instruction in various aspects of "leadership" that might be classed as public management if offered in other institutions. Admission to party schools is not based on the national entrance examinations, and state agencies have no direct role in their operation. However, since many students come from and will return to state agencies, it seems certain that officials in those organizations influence the selection of students and the content of specific courses. This influence is exercised through relevant party committees.

5

Institutions of Higher Education

In 1987, there were 1,063 regular institutions of higher education in China; 161 of these had been established since 1985, signaling continuation of the trend that began almost immediately after the death of Mao and the purge of the "Gang of Four" in late 1976. Since that time, the number of institutions of higher learning (an imprecise term that probably includes two- and three-year schools as well as four- and five-year institutions) has increased by more than 650, and total enrollment has more than quadrupled. The following table records the rapid growth in the number of institutions and somewhat slower increase in the number of students since 1949.*

Academic Year	Number of Tertiary-level Institutions	Number of Students
1949–50	205	117,000
1952–53	201	191,000
1953–54	181	212,000
1958–59	791	660,000
1965–66	434	674,000
1971–72	328	83,000
1975–76	387	501,000
1977–78	404	625,000
1978–79	598	856,000
1979–80	633	1,020,000
1980–81	675	1,144,000
1981–82	704	1,280,000
1982–83	715	1,154,000
1983–84	805	1,207,000
1984–85	902	1,328,400
1985–86	1,016	1,703,100
1986–87	1,063	2,064,900

*The figures from 1949–50 to 1983–84 are from *Higher Education in Europe*, July-September 1985; the figures from 1984–85 to 1986–87 were furnished by the State Education Commission.

Initial increases in the number of institutions were achieved by reopening schools that had been closed since the start of the Cultural Revolution in 1966, when there were 434 colleges and universities. Subsequent increases result from the reclassification and/or upgrading of secondary-level institutions, many of which specialize in teacher training. As an interesting comparision, it might be noted that while there were 704 tertiary-level institutions in China in 1982, the number of four-year institutions in the United States exceeded 700 in approximately 1900.

Ironically, college enrollments were much lower during the radically egalitarian period of the Cultural Revolution than in years before 1966 and after 1977. Rapid increases were possible after 1977 because existing facilities were underutilized and because, for a time, China experimented with day students and branch campuses. In addition, the shift back to four- and five-year programs led to large increases simply because students who previously would have graduated remained on campus. Slower rates of increase since 1979 have resulted from the fact that most institutions in China, and certainly a majority of the new schools, have small enrollments (1,000 or less). Nevertheless, freshmen enrollments increased by approximately 10,000 per year and graduate enrollments by an equal number between 1979 and 1982. And between 1984 and 1985, freshmen enrollments increased by 30.3 percent and graduate enrollments doubled—an indication of the importance placed on education by the Chinese government, which has allocated increased funds to education to permit the opening of an increased number of new institutions.

Types of Institutions

"Key" and "Ordinary" Institutions. Perhaps the most important distinction between different types of schools in China is that between "key" or "keypoint" universities and colleges and "ordinary" or "non-key" schools. Key institutions have the best faculties and facilities, enroll the most qualified students, and receive special support and financing. Although representatives of the Chinese government stated in 1986 that the concept of key institutions no longer exists, the term still is being used by Chinese educators, and special funding still is being provided to institutions that were designated key in the past. The most prestigious institutions are classified as "national key" institutions; these receive the greatest amount of funding and support.

At last report, there were 97 national key schools. Some national key institutions are supervised jointly by the State Education Commission and other ministry-level agencies; others are under the sole jurisdiction of the SEDC. Most of the institutions accorded keypoint status in 1978 (when the practice was revived) had enjoyed similar distinction before the Cultural Revolution. The reason for reviving the designation was essentially the same as that invoked when the classification was first used in the 1950s—the need to make optimal use of limited resources. There also are provincial key institutions, which are so designated by the Provincial Bureaus of Higher Education that oversee the specific educational needs of the province. Provincial key institutions receive preference for funding and support next after national key institutions.

Institutional Specialization. A second important distinction is that between comprehensive and specialized schools. China has relatively few comprehensive universities (defined by the SEDC as institutions with schools or faculties of both "science" and "liberal arts"). These schools do not offer as broad a range of programs as do similar universities in the United States, and they are not as comprehensive as were the foreign-organized schools of pre-1949 China, even though many of the current comprehensive universities are direct descendants of schools founded by foreign colleges and/or religious organizations. During the 1950s, when China adopted a Soviet-style system of higher education (a system marked by narrow specialization), several comprehensive schools were subdivided into separate specialized colleges. Narrow specialization is now regarded as a serious problem by some Chinese educators, who observe that many advances in science, engineering, and public policy have resulted from inter- and cross-disciplinary research and training of a kind that is difficult, if not impossible, in many Chinese institutions.

Although reforms currently are under way to broaden courses offered by many institutions of higher education, it still is possible and useful at the present time to distinguish among the following types of institutions (there are key and ordinary institutions in each category).

Comprehensive Universities. Approximately four percent of China's 1,063 institutions of higher learning (47) are classified as "comprehensive" universities offering programs in both the sciences (basic and/or applied) and the arts (social sciences and/or humanities). Although this category includes such prestigious national key institutions as Beijing, Fudan, Nanjing, and Zhongshan universities, it also includes a number of provincial universities (e.g., Shandong and Sichuan universities) that have not been designated national key schools. Despite the seemingly unambiguous criteria specified above, one school in this category (China People's University) does not offer programs in engineering or the basic sciences.

Polytechnical Universities. Institutions in this category have curricula that cover a broad range of applied sciences and engineering subjects, but do not offer full or formal programs in the humanities or social sciences. Leading polytechnical institutions include Qinghua, Tongji, Zhejiang, and Shanghai Jiaotong universities. While some schools in this category are administered solely by the State Education Commission and/or its subordinate bureaus, others fall under the joint jurisdiction (or dual leadership) of the SEDC and another ministry-level agency. For example, Shanghai Jiaotong University is subordinate to both the SEDC and the State Shipbuilding Corporation, and China University of Science and Technology is under the dual authority of the SEDC and the Chinese Academy of Sciences. The 272 polytechnical universities constitute approximately 26 percent of all tertiary-level institutions.

Institutions of Science and Technology. Schools in this category offer specialities or majors in relatively few (roughly 3 to 12) engineering or basic science fields. The size and quality of these schools vary widely, but most are smaller than the comprehensive and polytechnical universities, and some (perhaps most) have fewer than 1,000 students. The degree of specialization often is indicated by the name (e.g., Beijing College of Aeronautics, East China Petroleum Institute, and the Jiangsu College of Chemical Engineering). Most of the institutions in this category are administered jointly by the SEDC and another ministry, such as the Ministry of Chemical Industry or the Ministry of Energy.

Teacher-Training (Normal) Institutions. Normal schools and colleges, which are responsible for training teachers in China, consist mainly of teachers colleges and universities and teachers secondary schools. Teachers colleges and universities are divided into two groups: those that offer a four-year regular college course and those that provide a two- or three-year professional training course. The former, usually called teachers universities or teachers colleges, are engaged in training middle-school teachers; the latter, often called senior normal schools, train teachers for junior middle-schools. Students in both groups are senior middle-school graduates. Teachers secondary schools, including both general ones and those that train teachers for minority nationalities, preschool, foreign language, and special education, usually enroll junior middle-school graduates; they offer a three- to four-year program, and train teaching staff for primary schools and kindergartens.

In 1987, there were 260 teachers colleges and universities in China, approximately 24 percent of the total number of postsecondary institutions. The 253 normal colleges and universities that existed in 1985 had a total enrollment of 421,600 and a full-time teaching staff of 66,000 (figures are not available for 1987). In 1985, there were 1,028 teachers secondary schools, with a total enrollment of 558,200 and a full-time teaching staff of 46,000.

Teachers colleges and universities are ordered in a hierarchy with the two national key normal universities (Beijing Normal University and East China Normal University in Shanghai) at the top and municipal normal schools at the bottom. Regional key and provincial teachers colleges/normal schools occupy intermediate points on the hierarchy. Generally speaking, Beijing and East China Normal universities train students to teach at provincial teachers colleges and/or to conduct research on topics related to education; relatively few graduates teach in secondary schools. The regional key normal schools (i.e., Northeast Normal in Jilin, Northwest Normal in Xi'an, Southwest Normal in Chongqing, Central South Normal in Guangzhou, and Central Normal in Wuhan) train individuals to teach in provincial normal schools within the region served by each school as well as in secondary schools.

In addition to increasing the number of qualified teachers by offering training in teachers colleges, universities, and secondary schools, China is also attempting to improve the level of competency of the eight million primary- and middle-school teachers currently working in schools by providing in-service training. Correspondence schools are run by teachers colleges and universities, and a teacher-training network at the provincial, prefectural, and county levels has been established. In 1985, there were 216 colleges of education or teachers continuation schools throughout the country, with a total enrollment of 247,100 and a full-time teaching staff of 20,700. Also, there were 1,848 county-level teachers re-training schools, with a total enrollment of 684,200 and a full-time teaching staff of 27,800. Colleges of education or teachers continuation schools at provincial levels mainly train teachers and administrators for senior middle-schools; those at prefectural levels train teachers and administrators for junior middle-schools; county-level teachers re-training schools train teachers for primary schools.

Several new programs were instituted in 1985 to train teachers. Cadres from central party and government departments are being sent to the provinces to train local primary- and middle-school teachers. Teacher-training courses are being established at colleges and universities that do not normally offer such courses. The enrollment system in teachers colleges and universities, based on provinces, autonomous regions, and municipalities, is being reformed so they can recruit new students in advance of the unified college entrance examinations or have priority in admitting students ahead of other types of colleges after the unified college entrance examinations. Finally, a special television channel has been opened through satellite transmission to offer teacher-training courses.

In addition, in January 1988 the State Education Commission announced that teachers in primary and middle schools will be given qualification examinations. Those who fail will be assigned to other jobs. As reported, China's 8.2 million primary and middle school teachers have until 1991 to pass the exam and obtain teaching qualification certificates. The SEDC reported that of 5.4 million primary-school teachers, 37 percent lack the required two years of higher education; of 2.23 million junior middle-school teachers, 70 percent do not have the required three years.

Medical Schools. These are administered jointly by the State Education Commission and the Ministry of Public Health. Most focus on Western medicine, but also teach some Chinese traditional practices. Few specialize in Chinese traditional medicine. Students enter medical programs in China after graduation from secondary school; to become a physician or dentist requires five years of instruction followed by an internship. Some medical schools offer advanced training in specialities, such as cardiology. In 1987, there were 120 medical schools in China, 11 percent of all postsecondary-level institutions.

Agricultural Schools. Universities, colleges, and schools of agriculture are administered jointly by the SEDC and the Ministry of Agriculture (or its subordinate bureaus). The 61 agricultural schools constitute about 6 percent of the total. The breadth and quality of instruction appear to vary widely depending on the status of the institution (i.e., whether it is a national or provincial institution, and whether or not it has graduate students).

Law Schools. In 1987, there were 25 institutions of political science and law. There were 42,034 undergraduate students specializing in this field; but all of these students may not be attending the 25 institutions of political science and law, since some comprehensive universities, such as Beijing University and the People's University of China, also have departments of political science and law. Just as in medical schools, instruction in law begins at the undergraduate level, with the first degree being the bachelor's degree.

Specialized Non-Technical Institutions. This catch-all category subsumes the 170 schools of finance and trade, commerce, politics and law, foreign languages, music, fine arts, physical education, and minority affairs—approximately 16 percent of the total. The schools in each subgroup are few in number, and have relatively few (1,000 or less) students. Many institutions in this category are administered jointly by the SEDC and another ministry-level agency, such as the Ministry of Commerce or the Ministry of Culture.

Research Institutes of the Chinese Academy of Sciences and the Chinese Academy of Social Sciences. A small number of graduate students (totaling perhaps as many as a few thousand) are enrolled not in universities but in research institutes administered by the Chinese Academy of Sciences (CAS) or the Chinese Academy of Social Sciences (CASS). These students are selected through the graduate (postgraduate) entrance examinations administered by the SEDC, but their programs are solely or primarily designed by the academies. In the case of the CASS, all graduate students are enrolled in the Graduate School of the CASS and attend classes at the campus in Beijing. (Faculty are drawn from affiliated institutes, all of which are located in Beijing.) The CAS administers (together with the SEDC) the Graduate School of the Chinese University of Science and Technology in Beijing, but not all CAS students are on the campus of that facility. Many receive advanced and highly specialized instruction in the institutes of the Academy of Sciences. The CAS (and/or its subordinate institutes) and the CASS are authorized to confer degrees in accordance with the regulations approved by the State Council in 1981.

Other Research Institutes. In addition to the institutes administered by the CAS and the CASS, China has hundreds of other research and training facilities. Little is known about the level of instruction provided. Some tertiary-level training probably does occur, but too little is known to make even general statements about the quality of these programs. Students/trainees are not known to be admitted through the national entrance examinations, and may be admitted after lower middle-school.

Military Institutions of Higher Education. Tertiary-level institutions run by the Ministry of Defense enroll perhaps 60,000 students. The precise number of schools in this category is unknown, but 22 key military schools of higher learning were reported in mid-1980. Judging by the names of the key schools (e.g., the Advanced Ordnance School, the Armored Technical Institute, and the Signal Engineering Institute) curricula are highly specialized. Students are not known to be selected through the national entrance examinations.

Profiles of Chinese tertiary-level institutions can be found in *Higher Education and Research in the People's Republic of China: Institutional Profiles*, produced by the U.S.-China Education Clearinghouse in 1981. A microfiche copy can be ordered from the ERIC Documentation Reproduction Service, 3900 Wheeler Avenue, Alexandria, VA 22304. The National Association for Foreign Student Affairs produced an update to this publication, *China Update #5: Profiles of Chinese Postsecondary Institutions*, in 1984.

Radio and Television Universities, Spare-Time Universities. In addition to the "regular" colleges and universities that admit students on the basis of the national entrance examinations, China has a variety of "irregular" or alternative schools, including radio and television universities and spare-time universities.

Radio and Television Universities. China's Central Radio and Television University was founded in Beijing in February 1979. At the same time, radio and television university campuses were established in all Chinese provinces, autonomous regions, and municipalities except Tibet and Taiwan. In 1984, there were 29 radio and television universities, including the one run by the central government, and approximately 600 branch institutes at the municipal or prefectural level and in various trades and industries, as well as 1,100 small groups at the county level. In addition, there were over 20,000 study classes in enterprises, government organs, and organizations that constituted part of the nationwide network of higher education for radio and television. In 1984, radio and television universities had a teaching staff of 23,000, of which 11,000 were full-time teachers. The total student enrollment was 600,000; students learning by audiovisual means numbered 400,000.

Radio and television universities at various levels are under the direct leadership of governments at corresponding levels. The Central Radio and Television University is a higher education institution directed jointly by the State Education Commission and the Ministry of Radio and Television, whereas radio and television universities of the various provinces, municipalities, and autonomous regions are higher education institutions under governments at corresponding levels. Branch institutes or groups in various places, trades, and industries are affiliated with their respective authorities. Radio and television institutes at various levels have a relationship of professional guidance, the higher level guiding the next lower level. Administratively, radio and television universities at various levels are in charge of administrative departments at corresponding levels. Operating expenses also are allocated by these departments. Funds for conducting study classes are provided by sponsoring units.

Since 1979, the following departments and specialities (listed in parentheses) have been developed: science (mathematics, physics, and chemistry); engineering (machine building, electricity, chemical industry, civil engineering, and management engineering); economics (operation and management of industrial enterprises, operation and management of commercial enterprises, industrial accounting, commercial accounting, industrial statistics, finance, banking, and economic management of materials); and liberal arts (language and literature, journalism, law, library science, archives, and basic knowledge for party and government cadres). Altogether, there are 22 specialities offering 158 courses. (It was planned to establish five new specialities in 1986 in economic management of labor, economic management of tourism, economic administration of personnel, auditing, and finance of capital construction.) Courses of study require two or three years.

China's radio and television universities use a combination of radio, television, and correspondence. Courses in science and engineering departments are given chiefly on television, complemented by radio and correspondence, and courses in liberal arts and economics departments are given mainly by radio, complemented by television and correspondence.

Because a limited number of homes have television sets, television university classes are scheduled in "classrooms" in various government buildings, including university buildings. Courses are broadcast more than 30 hours per week. Each week, extra classes are scheduled by "coaches" who are available to explain difficult points or provide individual assistance. These coaches include teachers from municipal universities and industries. Undergraduate students also serve as coaches. (The dependence on these coaches is emphasized by the fact that nearly 1,000 such coaches serve 12,000 students in the television branch of Shanghai's Spare-Time University.) Until recently, no special training was given to the coaches; several universities now provide preparatory sessions before or while courses are offered.

In teaching and administration, China's radio and television universities follow a principle of "unified planning, administration by authorities at various levels, and the establishment of courses on three tiers." There is a division of labor between radio and television universities at various levels regarding the establishment of courses. The Central Radio and Television University offers basic courses and specialized basic courses for general purposes. Local radio and television universities offer some specialized basic and other courses to meet their own needs. Lessons given by the Central Radio and Television University are relayed nationwide through a microwave hookup, while general radio lessons are broadcast by local radio stations. Parts of the lessons are made into cassettes or videotapes for distribution to radio and television universities at various levels. Courses are taught by teachers who are experienced, of high academic level, and from noted universities throughout the country. Course content is at the university level.

Students of radio and television universities enter through examinations—studying in classes full time, part time, or during their spare time—or study by themselves from radio and television without sitting the entrance examinations. Entrance examinations are administered once each term by the radio or television university to which the applicant is applying. Individual exams are given for each subject; an applicant takes only the exam for the subject he or she wishes to study.

Students include workers, school teachers, technicians, government functionaries, individuals who did not have a chance to study during the Cultural Revolution, and unemployed individuals. They do not have to be middle-school graduates. Tuition and fees for student-workers admitted to radio and television universities are paid by employers. Student-workers who attend radio and television universities on a full-time basis are released from their work unit but continue to receive full wages and health and housing benefits; they return to their work units after completion of their studies.

To test study-results, an examination is held at the end of each term on a fixed day at educational institutions throughout the country. The test papers are prepared by the Central Radio and Television University and graded by local proctors according to standard criteria. China's radio and television universities use the credit system. Students gain credits after passing the examination. When they have collected the required number of credits for graduation or completion of a certain subject, they are awarded diplomas or certificates. Students who study by themselves from radio and television without sitting the entrance examinations also may apply to take part in examinations of some subjects given by the university. Those who pass the examinations also are granted certificates for completing a certain subject or graduation diplomas. Individuals who receive graduation diplomas from radio and television universities are considered by the Chinese government to have an education equivalent to that of three-year college graduates.

Between 1979 and 1984, China's radio and television universities enrolled 1,400,000 students. In addition, hundreds of thousands of students attended radio and television lectures at home or at their places of work. Thus, in the first six years of existence, radio and television universities have provided opportunities for two million individuals to receive higher education. There have been three graduating classes, totaling 340,000 students. An additional 400,000 individuals have completed the study of a certain subject.

The Chinese government has attached great importance to the development of radio and television universities. It planned to launch a radio satellite in 1986 that would have had one station devoted exclusively to education, thus increasing the hours of radio lessons. It also planned to build UHF educational transmitting stations in nine cities and establish 85 study centers. Loans have been extended by the World Bank for promoting radio and television universities in China. A large increase in the number of specialities and courses also is planned so that by 1990 the number of courses offered will reach 200. It is anticipated that by the 1990s, one out of every three college students in China will be a student of a radio and television university.

Spare-Time Universities. The number of spare-time universities has grown dramatically since 1982. Most are night schools run by private individuals. If such individuals have extra rooms in their house and want to start a spare-time university, they apply to the local (district) government for a license, hire teachers (usually from local universities), and buy desks, chairs, and other equipment needed. Rooms at local primary and secondary schools also might be used for such universities. All expenses involved with spare-time universities (salaries of teachers, electricity and heat expenses, etc.) are paid by the individual running the institution. That individual charges tuition fees to students to cover these expenses.

Anyone can be a student at a spare-time university. There are no entrance examinations or age limits; students simply must be able to pay the tuition fee. Persons organizing spare-time universities advertise in local newspapers, using the "official" name adopted by the institution, to recruit students.

Generally, courses are given Monday through Friday evenings and Sunday afternoons. There are beginning and advanced classes, and in some cases, such as English, university textbooks are used. Students who complete courses at spare-time universities are awarded completion certificates.

Summary

Although the State Education Commission has ultimate responsibility for all 1,063 regular colleges and universities, it exercises direct supervisory authority over relatively few. Provincial bureaus of higher education and numerous other ministry-level agencies play a more direct role in the operation of most tertiary-level institutions than does the SEDC. Still, the power to approve budgets gives SEDC officials a very influential voice in all aspects of China's higher education. Nevertheless, the impossibility of managing an educational system in the manner suggested by idealized organization charts and formal regulations has led to necessary and constructive "compromises" between the SEDC and its constituent units. Colleges and universities have recovered a fair amount of de facto autonomy, especially outside Beijing, and further reform of the basic organizational structure has been mandated by the 1985 educational reform document and the Seventh Five-Year Plan (1986–90) approved by the Fourth Plenary Session of the Sixth National People's Congress in April 1986.

6
Selection Procedures and Academic Programs

Introduction

Admission to one of China's 1,063 regular colleges and universities is highly competitive, with the millions of students who begin primary school dwindling to thousands at the graduate level. (See accompanying chart.)

College graduates constitute a tiny minority of the total population. As was true during the period prior to the Cultural Revolution, higher education is perhaps the primary path to power and prestige. Career-minded young people and their families set their sights on the 600,000 annual openings at the tertiary level. In recent years, more than two million middle-school graduates and other young people have taken the national entrance examinations, so competition is indeed fierce. Although the central government attempts to mitigate the sense of competition and anxiety surrounding the selection process by offering alternatives to regular college programs (e.g., correspondence, radio, and television courses, spare-time educational opportunities, and, most recently, a small number of "private" colleges that charge tuition but about which little is known), most people regard admission to regular programs as the only desirable option. Those who make it through the various stages of the selection process represent the best of a very large pool of applicants. The pages that follow describe the selection process and typical student programs.

National Entrance Examinations

Prior to the Cultural Revolution, China subscribed to the dictum that "everyone is equal before the marks." Accordingly, admission to tertiary-level schools was based on competitive examinations prepared and administered by the Ministry of Education. These tests were designed to measure academic achievement. Those who achieved the best scores

PRC Educational Track (1985)*

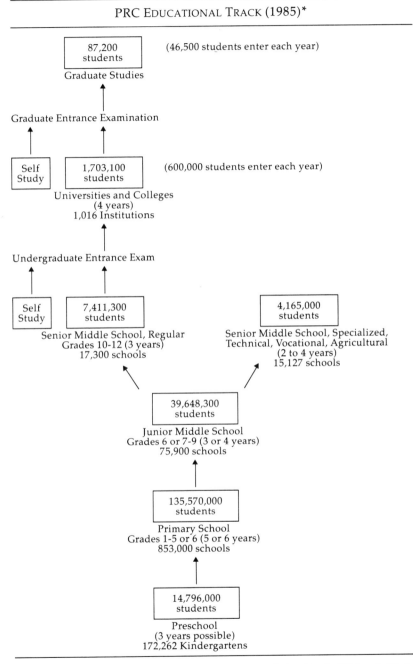

87,200 students
Graduate Studies

(46,500 students enter each year)

Graduate Entrance Examination

Self Study

1,703,100 students
Universities and Colleges
(4 years)
1,016 Institutions

(600,000 students enter each year)

Undergraduate Entrance Exam

Self Study

7,411,300 students
Senior Middle School, Regular
Grades 10-12 (3 years)
17,300 schools

4,165,000 students
Senior Middle School, Specialized,
Technical, Vocational, Agricultural
(2 to 4 years)
15,127 schools

39,648,300 students
Junior Middle School
Grades 6 or 7-9 (3 or 4 years)
75,900 schools

135,570,000 students
Primary School
Grades 1-5 or 6 (5 or 6 years)
853,000 schools

14,796,000 students
Preschool
(3 years possible)
172,262 Kindergartens

* This chart is based upon one compiled in 1980 by Karlene N. Dickey (Stanford University) that has been updated with 1985 SEDC statistics.

on these tests were admitted to undergraduate programs of four to five years' duration (except for programs in medicine and a few other fields which required six to eight years for the first degree). Postgraduate education was very limited; only 16,000 were trained at the graduate level in the 17 years before the Cultural Revolution. Upon completion of their programs, graduate students received certificates rather than diplomas.

The education system generally and the admissions process in particular were severely criticized during the Cultural Revolution. College-level instruction ceased entirely between 1966 and 1971; when schools reopened in 1971–72, they were dramatically different from the past. Admissions tests were revived, but radical criticism prevented effective utilization of the results. "Class background" and nomination by one's work unit were accorded greater importance than was intellectual prowess. Two or more years of productive labor following middle school was required before entrance to college. College programs, for the most part reduced to two or three years, included a great deal of political study, manual work, and production-oriented training, with little emphasis on basic science, humanities, or traditional academic subjects.

Efforts to improve the quality of higher education began in the early 1970s, but were thwarted by those now denounced under the sobriquet of the "Gang of Four." Indeed, it was in the realm of education, particularly higher education, that the "Gang" was most disruptive. After the downfall of this group in October 1976, the new leadership moved promptly to restore the country's colleges and universities. One of the first steps taken in this effort was revitalization of the entrance examinations.

In 1977, the government announced that college students would be selected on a new basis: entrance examinations would be reinstated, and candidates would be selected from among those who had just graduated from senior middle-school. Thus, university admissions would be determined in much the same way as before the Cultural Revolution. The 1977 National Conference on Enrollment Work led to the establishment of enrollment committees in each province charged with determining the content and assessing the results of college entrance examinations administered in the province. These provincial tests followed national guidelines and were regarded as transitional expedients to be replaced in 1978 by national examinations.

The October 1977 entrance examinations consisted of three common subjects (mathematics, politics, and Chinese language) and one additional subject depending on the intended area of study. Social science students took history/geography and science, and engineering students took physics/chemistry; each subject was scored on the basis of 100, giving a total maximum mark of 400. These examinations did not test proficiency in a foreign language. A total of 5.7 million people took the college entrance examinations in October 1977; 283,000 enrolled in institutions of higher learning in late spring 1978. In contrast to classes enrolled between 1971 and 1977, this new class entered programs lasting four, and in a few cases five, years.

The 1977 provincial entrance examinations were faulted for their insufficient emphasis on recruiting the best qualified students, lack of standardization nationally, and insufficient effort to inform students about opportunities to study outside their home provinces.

The first new national college entrance examinations were held in July 1978. Questions were drafted by the Ministry of Education; throughout China, all tests were given on the same days and hours, and in the same sequence. However, individual provinces administered the exams and assessed the results. Similar procedures have been followed since. The number taking the test declined from six million in 1978 to 2.5 million in the mid-1980s as eligibility requirements were tightened to limit the applicant pool. One quarter of the persons taking the exams—600,000 to 700,000 students—are admitted annually to Chinese institutions of higher education.

On April 24, 1987, the State Education Commission issued the "Provisional Regulations for Enrollment of Regular Institutions of Higher Learning." These regulations do not substantially change past policy, since colleges and universities supposedly have considered applicants based on political and physical suitability as well as academic preparation since at least the 1950s. However, they indicate to institutions that adherence to government policy will be more strictly enforced. The regulations include the following provisions.

In recruiting students, regular institutions of higher learning must implement the principle of enrolling students through all-around assessment of the candidates' political, intellectual, and physical qualities and of admitting the best qualified candidates into college. Those who are eligible in these respects will be chosen according to state plans and standard nationwide entrance examinations.

Chinese citizens who meet the following requirements may take part in the entrance examinations for regular institutions of higher learning: (1) they must support the "four cardinal principles," love the motherland, observe discipline and the laws, and express determination to study hard for the socialist modernization program; (2) they must be senior middle-school graduates or have achieved the same educational level; (3) they must be in good health and unmarried; and (4) they must be under 25—or under 23 for those who apply for

63

entrance to foreign language colleges or departments (except for various departments of teachers' colleges).

With the recommendation of the unit where they work, and with the approval of the college admission committee of the province, autonomous region, or municipality directly under the central government, outstanding young people with rich practical experience may have their age limit extended to 28. There is no age limit for those with special contributions. They may be either single or married. The college admission committee of any province, autonomous region, or municipality directly under the central government may decide to lower the admission threshold for candidates who meet the above-mentioned conditions and let the school select the best qualified for admission.

Enrollment in regular institutions of higher learning is divided into the following three forms: state assignment, students financed by the unit where they will be placed after graduation, and students studying at their own expense. (It was reported that in 1987 some 51,000 students would be financed by the units where they will placed after graduation and 5,800 students would study at their own expense.) The admission threshold for students studying at their own expense is lower than for applicants supported by the state or work units.

In dealing with candidates who have been found qualified through the assessment of their political, ideological, and moral qualities, who have passed the physical test, and whose grades in the unified entrance examination are above the control mark, the college or university may decide by itself whether to review the candidate's file and admit him or her. The college admission committee of any province, autonomous region, or municipality directly under the central government exercises supervision.

In order to implement the party's educational policy, teach students at their level of aptitude, and compensate for any shortcomings in the examination process, institutions of higher learning will be empowered by the state to enroll students who are recommended by schools but who have not sat for the examinations. In addition to the 46 institutions of higher learning and normal colleges that were empowered by the State Education Commission in 1987, senior middle-schools in Sichuan and Fujian provinces have been authorized to recommend, on a trial basis, students with all-around political, intellectual, and physical development to institutions of higher learning without taking examinations. Some senior middle-schools, considered by provincial-level educational departments to have qualified teaching staff, also may send selected graduates to local institutions of higher learning with the appropriate approval even though those students did not qualify in the national examinations.

Beginning in 1988, institutions of higher learning examine the social practice and physical educaiton of senior middle-school graduates in evaluating qualifications. Students who have not participated in social practice or who have failed to meet the standards for physical education (with the exception of those students who are exempt from taking physical education courses) are not qualified as candidates for regular institutions of higher learning.

A special reform was initiated in Shanghai beginning in 1987–88. Tests are being administered to high-school students to qualify for graduation from high school. The students who pass these examinations are required to take college entrance examinations in only four subjects: Chinese and mathematics (both compulsory) and two other subjects related to the major field of study. These examinees are unable to compete for admission to institutions outside Shanghai. If this experiment succeeds, other provinces may follow the example.

Selection and Placement

Undergraduate Students. Since 1978, the unified national entrance examinations have been classified in two groups: (1) six subjects for candidates of liberal arts—politics, Chinese, mathematics, history, geography, and foreign language (English, Russian, Japanese, French, German, or Spanish); and (2) seven subjects for candidates of natural science (science and engineering, agriculture, forestry, and medicine)—politics, Chinese, mathematics, physics, chemistry, biology (which was added in 1981), and foreign language (English, Russian, Japanese, French, German, or Spanish). The unified examinations are administered annually on July 7, 8, and 9. The time limit for each examination is two hours (with the exception of Chinese, which is two and one-half hours, and biology, which is one hour). The timing of the examinations for all subjects is as follows:

July 7: Morning—Chinese; Afternoon—chemistry/geography.
July 8: Morning—mathematics; Afternoon—politics/biology.
July 9: Morning—physics/history; Afternoon—foreign language.

Students pay two to three yuan to take the National College Entrance Examinations; the state pays 12 yuan per student for these exams. (The official exchange rate in June 1988 was Y2.79 = U.S. $1.)

The printing and distribution of the higher entrance examinations are administered by the working committees of higher-school enrollment of all provinces, municipalities, and autonomous regions. Examination sites are located in cities of county level or above; all aspects of the examination process are strictly regulated. There are approximately 53,000 examination sites in the more than 2,400 counties, cities, and districts throughout China. The administration of the examinations is monitored by more than 100,000 individuals.

The overall principle followed by the State Education Commission in determining questions for the examinations is that the examinations must be both advantageous to the selection of enrollees for institutions of higher education and conducive to the improvement of the level of teaching in middle schools. There are four factors involved, as follows:

1. Examinations must have a high forecast validity. They are not solely an achievement examination, but a means of selecting slightly more than one-fourth of middle-school graduates for entrance into institutions of higher education. Therefore, many of the questions must be more difficult than those of senior middle-school graduation examinations. Emphasis is placed on testing the basic knowledge and skills that the examinee learned in middle school and his or her ability to apply that knowledge in an actual life setting (i.e., both knowledge and ability are tested). In the Chinese language examination, for example, the questions are designed to test the student's reading comprehension, writing skills, and basic knowledge of contemporary Chinese language; reading comprehension and writing constititute 50 points each, and basic knowledge, 20 points. In the mathematics, physics, and chemistry examinations, questions are designed to test the examinee's basic knowledge and skill; ability to analyze, reason, calculate correctly and quickly; and ability to apply this knowledge comprehensively.

2. The scope of examination questions must not exceed the syllabuses of the subject for middle-school students or that of middle-school textbooks, but should include as much as possible of the basic contents of the middle-school syllabuses and textbooks as well as requirements for basic skills. For example, in the chemistry examination paper of 1984, 18 percent of the questions were from the third-year junior-middle-school textbooks, 40 percent were from the first volume of senior-middle-school texts, and 42 percent were from the second volume. The test paper included 50 concepts and over 80 elemental compounds, which covered all the basic theories in senior-middle-school textbooks, including physical constructions, periods laws of elements, chemical balance, and chemical calculations.

3. Examinations must include a suitable gradation of difficulty in order to distinguish the best students and to indicate the difference in the high scorers' grasp of knowledge and their ability to put their

knowledge into practice.

4. Since middle schools in China are divided into key schools and ordinary schools, which have different requirements, some optional questions of greater difficulty and higher level than the requirements of the middle-school syllabuses were added in 1984 to the examination papers in mathematics, physics, chemistry, English, and Russian. The optional questions for each subject add up to ten points; they are not added to the total score, but are intended for the reference of the higher education institutions admitting freshman enrollees.

The State Education Commission has been making continuous improvements in examination content and process. In addition to including traditional questions—true or false, fill-in-the-blanks, multiple choice, fill-in-the-pictures, read-the-pictures, calculations, definition of terms, correct-mistakes, answer-simple-questions, and comprehensive experiments—new efforts are made each year to upgrade the effectiveness of the examinations. More attention currently is being given to the standardization of examination questions, the objectivity of grading, and the modernization of the entire testing system.

In drafting examination papers, two sets of questions of roughly the same level are prepared for each subject (Set A and Set B), together with their respective correct answers. Set B is prepared in the event that the examination must be postponed.

After the examinations are given, more than 100,000 readers grade them in a period of approximately two weeks. To effectively administer the grading of examinations and maintain unified standards of grading, all grading workshops are located in a small number of schools in each province or city. Usually, examination papers of a specific subject are sent to one school.

Grading is conducted by faculty of institutions of higher education and of middle schools. Normally, 70 percent are from universities and 30 percent from middle schools. Before grading begins, all examiners study the "keys to the questions" and the "standards of grading." Some trial grading is then conducted to train the teachers. In the process of grading, senior teachers check the work of each examination section. In addition, selected examinations of the graded papers are conducted by individuals designated by the enrollment committees of provinces, municipalities, and autonomous regions to eliminate all possible mistakes, omissions, and unfair markings and to ensure the quality of the grading work. Each examiner is in charge of one question, with composition and essay questions the joint responsibility of two examiners. Expenses of the grading process are covered by the national enrollment budget. Examination scores are confidential, accessible only to the examinees themselves, education authorities, and the institutions and departments to which the examinees apply for admission.

Students are permitted to apply for admission to two institutions of higher education, plus three more for reference. They can apply to two departments or specialities within each institution. Since these choices are used in making final assignments, the advice given to senior middle-school students is very important. Advisers and students must make a realistic appraisal of anticipated exam performance when listing preferred schools and departments. Choosing unrealistic options could lead to failure to gain admission anywhere unless the candidate indicates a willingness to accept arbitrary placement.

Decisions by institutions of higher education to accept applicants are made according to the standard regulations of the enrollment committees of the applicable province, municipality, or autonomous region. After examinations are graded, the State Education Commission determines the minimally acceptable scores for admission so the approximately ten percent more students than can eventually be enrolled are eligible for consideration by institutions of higher education. The total possible score on the examinations usually is above 600, but it may vary from year to year. The passing scores do vary annually to ensure proper balance between the number of qualified candidates and the number of places available. Colleges and universities then select their enrollees according to the order of preference in the students' applications and their scores on relevant subjects.

Minimum passing scores on individual tests are not set nationally, but performance on particular tests does enter into placement decisions. Above the fixed minimum total score, considerable discretion is given to individual schools, departments, and specialities in setting minimum scores on particular parts of the exam. Thus, there is wide variation of subscores among successful candidates. Individual test scores are available to Chinese students taking the exams; these can be requested by U.S. institutions. Certified individual test scores are not available, however.

Each province is allocated a specified number of places at national key and ordinary colleges and universities, both within and outside the province. This system results in some anomalous developments. For example, if a province exceeds its quota of seats in key universities, some high-scoring applicants from that province will be placed in ordinary schools while lower-scoring candidates from other provinces will be admitted to key institutions.

Candidates who achieve appropriate scores on the entrance examinations are given a physical checkup and political evaluation. Little information is available on how these criteria are applied, or on the number of applicants eliminated at this stage. The initial political assessment is made by the candidate's work unit or middle school and subsequently by college or university authorities. Judgments pertain only to the students' activities; class backgound and family political history are no longer overtly relevant in determining college enrollment. In 1978, the Communist Party Central Committee eliminated the categories and class designations that had been used to discriminate against certain individuals (e.g., the children or grandchildren of rich peasants). Discriminating against children of "rightists," "bad elements," landlords, and rich peasants was denounced as an "abnormality" and "imperfection" of the socialist system. Individual cases indicate that these guidelines generally are being followed. However, official guidelines still specify that candidates of worker/peasant origin should be given preference when they have "basically the same political, intellectual, and physical qualifications" as other candidates. The same applies to minority ethnic groups.

In summary, final placement involves three considerations: (1) student preferences; (2) institutional preferences and priorities—national key universities have first choice of candidates, followed by national ordinary and provincial key and ordinary universities, and then prefectural and municipal institutions; and (3) "cultural heritage." National guidelines relating to the latter consideration specify that a "certain measure of priority" should be given to "national minorities, overseas Chinese, and compatriots from Taiwan, Hong Kong, and Macao." Provincial colleges are to give consideration to people from areas with "weak educational foundations." Teacher-training facilities are encouraged to admit students from rural areas, and medical schools are to give preference to barefoot doctors. Agricultural and forestry schools are to recruit rural students, and schools specializing in geology, mining, and petroleum technology are to give preference to workers in these fields and their children. Statistics on the implementation of these guidelines are not currently available.

In an effort to overcome the shortcomings of the national entrance examinations, the State Education Commission beginning in 1987 permitted some institutions of higher education to admit a small number of students with excellent academic records solely on the basis of recommendations from senior middle-schools (i.e., they did not need to take the entrance examinations). In addition, some students with specialized skills or knowledge are considered for admission by institutions of higher education on the basis of recommendations rather than the national entrance examinations.

Graduate Students. Between 1949 and 1966, a total of 23,393 graduate students (called postgraduates by English-speaking Chinese) were enrolled; 16,397 of them graduated. Most of the graduate students enrolled by institutions of higher education before 1962 studied for two years to become teachers. In 1962, three-year graduate courses were instituted, including preparation of graduate theses. In 1966, because of the Cultural Revolution, all graduate education in China ceased. In October 1977, after the conclusion of the Cultural Revolution, steps were taken to restore the training of graduate students. Incomplete statistics from 27 provinces, autonomous regions, and municipalities indicate that more than 63,500 candidates registered for examinations to pursue graduate study in 1978.

After preliminary examinations and re-examinations, 210 institutions of higher education and 162 scientific research institutions enrolled a total of 10,708 graduate students in 1978. Because of a shortage of candidates, a combined total of 11,726 graduate students were enrolled in 1979 and 1980.

From January 1, 1981, when the Regulations of the People's Republic of China on the Granting of Academic Degrees came into effect (see Degrees Conferred, p. 79), to the end of 1985, institutions of higher education and scientific research institutions throughout China enrolled a total of 102,361 students studying for master's degrees and 5,000 students studying for doctoral degrees. In all, 35,000 students were granted master's degrees and 300 were granted Ph.D. degrees.

In April 1987, the State Education Commission announced that colleges, universities, and research institutions planned to enroll 41,000 students in master's degree programs. No specifics were given for doctoral degree candidates.

The nationwide enrollment of graduate students is under the organization, leadership, and approval of the State Education Commission. The time and content of examinations are fixed by the departments that enroll graduate students. Present enrollment of graduate students adheres to the following guidelines.

• Graduate education must follow the principle of "quality guarantee and study development." In devising their plans, institutions of higher education and research institutions must take into account the needs of the modernization drive, the State Council's provisions for institutions granting advanced degrees, their own disciplines and fields of specialization, and their tutorial capability, scientific research foundations, laboratory facilities, resources of books and data, accommodations availability, and financial resources.

• Institutions that have the State Council's approval to grant advanced degrees are permitted to enroll graduate students. If other institutions have the basic conditions for the enrollment of graduate students and their specific disciplines and specialities are in urgent need of development in China, they also are permitted to enroll graduate students at the master's degree level, provided they are examined by the relevant administrations and approved by the State Education Commission.

• Graduating students in regular colleges and universities may, six months prior to graduation and job assignment, register for postgraduate entrance examinations. Colleges and universities and industrial and mining enterprises, scientific research institutions, government offices, and army units are requested to support those qualified to take such examinations.

To be eligible for programs leading to the master's degree, candidates must be graduates of regular colleges and universities, be in good health, and be under 35 years of age. For doctoral degrees, candidates must have received a master's degree or have an equivalent academic record, be in good health, and generally be under 40 years of age. In addition, doctoral candidates must be recommended by two experts above the rank of associate professor (or a corresponding title in a professional post) who are related to the specific discipline.

Entrance examinations for master's degree candidates cover five or six subjects, including political theory, foreign language, and specialized courses. Subjects for specialized courses are assigned by the institutions involved. The examinations are given in two stages, preliminary examinations and re-examinations. Preliminary examinations are closed-book written examinations. Re-examinations are a combination of oral and written tests. In 1984, the State Education Commission began a trial enrollment of master's degree candidates through recommendation and exemption from examination as well as through recommendation and examination. The number of candidates enrolled through recommendation and exemption from examination must be kept within five percent of the total number of master's degree candidates accepted in that year.

Doctoral candidates are examined in a foreign language and in specialized courses as determined by the institutions concerned. Entrance examinations for doctoral candidates are a combination of examinations (both written and oral) and recommendations.

Candidates for master's and doctoral degrees are assessed politically, intellectually, and physically. Only the best are admitted; quality, not quantity, is the important characteristic of graduate education.

71

Generally, there are no more than three master's degree candidates for each tutor and no more than two doctoral degree candidates for each tutor.

In 1987, the State Education Commission announced that candidates who had spent some time in the workforce since completing their undergraduate degrees would be given preference for postgraduate admissions. Further, applicants interested in fields such as philosophy and social and applied sciences were to be given priority. Since working graduate candidates would have less time to prepare for the entrance examinations than college students wishing to continue their education, it was decided to lower the passing marks for the first examinations. In addition, college graduates who had been admitted to study for master's degrees in 1987 were encouraged to work for one to three years before beginning graduate courses, the assumption being that a few years in the workforce improves the political awareness of college graduates and their ability to handle practical work.

Campus Life

The academic year is ten months long, and is made up of two semesters. The first term begins in late August or early September and ends at the beginning of Spring Festival or Lunar New Year in late January/early February. The second term begins in late February/early March, after a month-long holiday following Spring Festival, and runs through late June/early July. Classes are held six days per week.

Universities and other postsecondary institutions generally have large, impressive, self-contained campuses. Behind walls and through gates, one encounters secluded mini-cities. Most students live and eat within the campus; faculty and staff are housed on the campus as well, in apartment blocks. If a spouse works at another location, a choice may be made between the housing available on campus or at the spouse's worksite; but the overwhelming majority of the people connected with the institutions live within its walls. Thus, a university of 8,000 students could generate some 42,000 residents.

The university community might include primary and middle schools, a clinic or hospital, and stores. Many universities also have affiliated factories with an independent workforce. These factories often provide students the opportunity for practical training in an area related to their coursework. The income from the sale of factory-produced items occasionally is a source of additional discretionary funds for universities. In addition to academic departments, universities generally have a number of research institutes.

Living conditions for students are sparse, efficient, orderly, and clean. There is no privacy. Rooms are not large, measuring approximately 10 by 12 feet. Down each side of a room are bunk beds, two sets to a side or eight students to a room. Lined up and down the center of the room are very small study tables and chairs with overhead flourescent lights. Bathrooms and laundry rooms, where only washing by hand can be done as there are no machines, are communal. Students bring their own wash bowls—usually enameled metal in bright red, blue, and yellow. When not in use, the bowls are stacked neatly in students' rooms in a special rack tucked in the corner. Students also have smaller enamel bowls that they take to the cafeteria for meals, since they must supply their own eating utensils and plates or bowls. Clothes are magically stored out of sight. Heat is scarce, except in the far north, and hot water is available only periodically.

Chinese students must work, study, and live under very rigorous conditions. Study space, for example, is at a premium, so students make extraordinary use of the libraries. Yet most campus facilities close and classes stop for at least an hour each day so that all students can take part in some physical and recreational activity, such as track, volleyball, basketball, martial arts, jogging—whatever is of interest and available.

Foreign students are accepted only with the approval of the State Education Commission. When foreign students are accepted, they are given preferential treatment: for example, only two are assigned to a room, heat is more frequent, and hot water is available more often.

Academic Programs

Undergraduate. Undergraduate programs generally require four years of study; however, some specialities (majors), departments, and institutions require five years for a first degree. (For example, Qinghua University has a five-year first-degree program, and most medical schools require five years of instruction.) Undergraduates are admitted directly into a major department. For three years, they follow a prescribed course of study along with all other students majoring in the same department. In their final year, they select from a small number of "electives," but all those specializing in a particular subfield generally take the same elective courses. Courses in Chinese, foreign languages, basic math, and certain other introductory courses are taken together with students from other departments, but most courses are restricted to those in a particular department. The normal course load is five subjects per semester; each course meets daily for a 50-minute period. Interdepartmental courses are quite rare. Each course has a final exam, but there do not appear to be comprehensive subject

73

examinations. It is rare for undergraduate students to write research papers; the use of the library for purposes other than a place to study is uncommon.

Undergraduate courses emphasize both theory and basic subjects—a contrast to the "applied" or practical emphasis of courses offered during the later years of the Cultural Revolution. "Basics" now constitute at least two-thirds of the curriculum, and many subjects abolished during the Cultural Revolution have been restored.

The State Education Commission is responsible for preparing uniform textbooks for all subjects. Priority is being given to science and engineering subjects, but social science and humanities courses also are being standardized. Classes are large by U.S. standards, and are generally characterized by a passive atmosphere in which instructors lecture and students take notes. Relationships between students and teachers, and among students of the same year and department, are close and often of lifelong duration. This closeness often is reflected in the recommendations professors write for their students.

State Education Commission personnel note that in recent years theory has sometimes been divorced from practice in some colleges and universities. Therefore, the SEDC has called on institutions of higher education to strengthen practical training through various activities, including the following:

• Encouraging students to conduct social investigations in their home towns or villages during their vacations. Institutions assist students to establish objectives, select topics, design the framework, and acquire relevant skills and techniques. At the end of the investigation, students write a report about their experiences.

• Arranging for students to participate in work practice in both urban and rural areas (e.g., encouraging their use as consultants or their joining work/study programs).

• Extending students' vacations or shortening school terms to provide more time for practical training. Some institutions have adopted a three-semester system. In addition to introducing practical training, more optional courses and other courses that require fewer class hours have been initiated. Attention also has been given to the development of practical teaching activities.

Graduate. Graduate students studying for a master's degree take three or four basic-theory and specialized courses, spend two or three years in the study of Marxist theory and foreign languages, finish a master's thesis, pass examinations for required courses, successfully defend a thesis, have a firm command of basic theory and systematic specialized knowledge in their disciplines, and have the ability to conduct scientific research work or undertake specialized technical work. Upon fulfilling these qualifications, they are granted a master's degree.

Graduate students who take only required courses for a master's degree study for two years. Once they pass the examinations, they are permitted to graduate and are assigned jobs. They then finish the master's thesis at their work posts or write under the guidance of their tutors and successfully defend the thesis before being granted a master's degree.

Doctoral degree students usually spend three years beyond the two required for a master's degree in the study of basic-theory and specialized courses, two foreign languages, and Marxist theory, finish their doctoral thesis, pass the curricular examinations, and successfully defend their thesis. They are expected to be well grounded in basic theories and systematic specialized knowledge in their chosen fields and to have the ability to conduct independent research and achieve creative results in science or special technology. Upon fulfilling these qualifications, they are granted a doctoral degree.

To accelerate the training of senior specialized personnel, the State Education Commission instituted a system in 1984 whereby a small number of outstanding graduate students studying in colleges or universities for a master's degree could begin their study for a doctoral degree early. If they pass the qualification examinations, these students are permitted to study for a doctoral degree before completing a master's degree.

The training of graduate students usually combines the integration of theoretical study with scientific research under the guidance of tutors who have trained in teaching research sections. Every graduate student has a tutor, who is drawn from the ranks of professors, associate professors, or professionals with a corresponding title. Tutors work with the relevant teaching research sections to design a training program for each graduate student.

Graduate students released from work usually study nine months each year. Candidates for the master's degree spend at least half their study time on curricular studies. In most cases, they devote one to one-and-one-half years on research and the completion of the thesis. Doctoral candidates spend more time on research and less in classes. Graduate students at both levels usually spend one month or more in teaching practice. In-service graduate students may devote one-third or one-half their work time to study. If necessary, they may be released from work for six months to one year to write the thesis.

Curricula for graduate students are divided into required and elective courses. Required courses include a first foreign language, a second foreign language (for doctoral candidates), three or four basic-theory and specialized courses stipulated in the specialized training program, and Marxist theory. A number of elective courses can be selected if they expand the graduate student's range of knowledge and serve to update the student regarding advanced technology. With the permission of their tutors, graduate students may elect some courses outside their speciality, department, and/or institution of higher education. Examinations are conducted for both required and elective courses. The writing of a thesis is required for candidates of both master's and doctoral degrees.

Graduate students must pass the examinations for prescribed courses and an appraisal and examination of the thesis, and must successfully defend the thesis before they are granted an advanced degree approved by the academic degree appraisal committee of the institution of higher education or other institutions authorized to grant academic degrees. Graduate students who graduate from institutions not authorized to grant academic degrees may apply for a degree from an authorized institution; degrees may be granted to those who pass a series of examinations and successfully defend their thesis or dissertation.

National administration of enrollment, training, and other aspects of graduate education is under the planning and leadership of the State Education Commission. It is organized and carried out by the relevant administrations of bureaus/departments of higher education/education of the provinces, autonomous regions, and municipalities in compliance with the organizational relationships of the institutions of higher education and scientific research institutions.

Registration, examination, and admission of candidates for a master's degree are under the arrangement of the State Education Commission, organized and led by enrollment offices of institutions of higher education in various provinces, autonomous regions, and municipalities and carried out in collaboration with the institutions that enroll graduate students. Registration, examination, and admission of doctoral candidates are organized by the institutions that enroll graduate students.

Financial Support

No tuition charges or other fees have been levied at any of the 1,063 institutions supervised by the State Education Commission. However, it was reported in January 1988 that China was considering a tuition charge at all institutions of higher education, so the situation may change in the near future. Simultaneously, there is considerable discussion of replacing the current no-tuition policy with one of financial assistance based on a combination of financial need and academic ability.

Other expenses (such as food, books, laundry) are low in comparison to U.S. campuses, but they are substantial when measured against average incomes in China. For example, the average monthly expenditures of undergraduates (20 to 25 yuan or $11 to $14) equals approximately one-quarter of the average monthly earnings of urban workers and more than twice the monthly cash income of the average peasant. Financial aid sometimes is available to help offset these expenses.

The state provides monthly stipends to cover living and book expenses to students studying in teacher's colleges and universities and to students who will go to work under extremely hard conditions upon their graduation. Stipends are given regardless of need to induce young people to become teachers or to work at less desirable jobs. Scholarships are available for students with excellent academic performances, and grants-in-aid and loans are available to students who have financial difficulties.

Soon after the founding of the People's Republic of China, the state established a grant-in-aid system designed to develop the high-level specialists urgently needed in the country's construction and to help workers and peasants and their children enter colleges and assist with any financial problems during their years of study. However, because of the changes that have occurred in China's economy and society as well as the overall reforms of its economic and educational systems, the state grant-in-aid system has drawn increasing criticism in China. It is said to provide too much care for college students, thereby causing students to become too dependent on the state. Also, the awarding of grants solely on the basis of a student's family's financial situation, rather than the student's academic performance, is objectionable to some.

The state grant-in-aid system has been judged to have an adverse impact on efforts to encourage students to study hard. As a result, the State Council in July 1986 approved the Report on Reforming the Current State Grant-in-Aid System in General Institutions of Higher Learning, which had been jointly submitted by the State Education Commission and the Ministry of Finance. In 1986, 85 colleges and universities initiated experimental reforms in the state grant-in-aid system for new students. The original grant-in-aid system remained in effect for college students already enrolled.

Depending on results, new experiments were to be implemented in 1987. No information currently is available about what reforms actually occurred. After the state grant-in-aid system is reformed, it is planned to introduce both a scholarship system and a student loan system.

Scholarships would fall into three categories:

• Scholarships for superior students would be subdivided into three levels. Approximately five percent of the total enrollment would receive the first-level scholarship, which provides 350 yuan per student per year. Approximately ten percent of the students would receive the second-level scholarship of 250 yuan over a one-year period. Another ten percent would receive the third-level scholarship of 150 yuan over a one-year period.

• Scholarships for students in special majors who are enrolled by teachers, agricultural and forestry, sports, nationalities, marine transport, and other colleges and institutions would also be divided into three levels. The third-level scholarship of 300 yuan over one year would be provided to all first-year students. Beginning in the second year, approximately five percent of the students would qualify for the first-level scholarship of 400 yuan over one year, and ten percent would receive the second-level scholarship of 350 yuan over one year. The remaining 85 percent would continue to receive the third-level scholarship.

• Scholarships would be available to students who pledge to work in border areas or economically backward areas and in professions with poor work conditions after their graduation. No specific level of scholarship has been indicated.

The student loan system would assist some students who cannot afford part or all of the expenses at college. Each such student would receive a loan of 300 yuan per year, but the number of students receiving loans would be limited to 30 percent of the total college enrollment. The loans would be provided by the China Industrial and Commercial Bank annually at a low interest rate. Once the graduating students who have received loans are employed, their employers would repay the amount borrowed to the bank in a lump sum. After their probation period, the money would be deducted from the students' salaries each month over a five-year period. However, debts might be remitted with the approval of relevant authorities for students who, upon their graduation, go to work in primary or secondary schools or in former revolutionary bases, minority nationalities areas, mountainous areas, border areas, or economically backward areas, or in professions with poor conditions. Their debts would be repaid by the state with money from the operation budget of institutions approved by the central government.

If a graduate student is a full-time worker at the time of selection, the work unit pays all expenses, including a subsidy for family living expenses if necessary. Other graduate students, including recent undergraduates, currently are supported by the institution through a grant-in-aid equal to 90 percent of the wage earned by the average college graduate in the locality. (This also may be affected by the proposed reforms in the state grant-in-aid system.) Those graduate students selected by the State Education Commission for study abroad receive a modest living stipend as well as money to cover tuition and fees. All students studying abroad are strongly encouraged to seek alternative sources of support, such as fellowships from foreign institutions or money from relatives living outside China.

Degrees Conferred

Before the founding of the People's Republic of China in 1949, very few academic degrees were granted in China. Most were bachelor's degrees (some universities granted a limited number of master's degrees). After 1949, several attempts to institute a different degree system were thwarted by successive political movements.

New Regulations Concerning Academic Degrees in the People's Republic of China became effective on January 1, 1981. A Committee on Academic Degrees of the State Council was appointed to design measures for the implementation of the regulations and submit them to the State Council for approval. On May 20, 1981, the Provisional Measures for the Implementation of the Regulations Concerning Academic Degrees in the People's Republic of China were approved by the State Council.

In June 1981, the Committee on Academic Degrees of the State Council authorized a 407-member appraisal board to oversee the granting of degrees. The first group of higher education institutions was authorized to confer master's and doctoral degrees in 1981; conferral of bachelor's degrees began in 1982. China opted for a unified system similar to that used in Japan and the Soviet Union to define disciplines in which degrees are awarded, rather than the U.S. or British system in which the disciplines are defined by the universities conferring degrees.

Bachelor's, master's, and doctoral degrees are conferred in ten disciplines: philosophy, economics, law, education, literature, history, natural sciences, engineering, agriculture, and medicine. Literature includes linguistics, art, and library science; law includes political science, sociology, and ethnology; education includes physical culture.

In order to maintain the standards in degree courses, only selected colleges and universities have been authorized to grant degrees. By 1984, 460 institutions had been authorized to award bachelor's degrees. At the end of 1985, there were 425 institutions authorized to award master's degrees, including 320 institutions of higher education and 105 scientific research institutions. There were 196 institutions authorized to issue doctoral degrees, including 155 institutions of higher education and 41 scientific research institutions. (A list of these institutions as of 1984, with the number of specialities in which degrees are conferred, is included in the NAFSA publication *China Update #5: Profiles of Chinese Postsecondary Institutions.*)

To ensure the academic quality of students receiving degrees, units authorized to confer degrees have formed academic-degree evaluation committees as well as panels for conducting interviews on the theses for academic degrees in various disciplines. The panels are responsible for examining the master's and doctoral theses, organizing interviews, making decisions on conferring the master's or doctoral degrees, and reporting these decisions to the Academic Degree Evaluation Committee. The Academic Degree Evaluation Committee, which is composed of from 9 to 25 members who serve a term of two to three years, is responsible for examining and approving the name list of those receiving the bachelor's degree and the name list submitted by the panels for conducting theses interviews and making decisions on granting master's, doctoral, and honorary doctoral degrees. Once the decisions have been made, this committee annually submits the number of winners of the bachelor's degree, the lists of winners of the master's and doctoral degrees, and other related materials to both the governmental department in charge and the Academic Degree Committee of the State Council, where they are kept on record.

Bachelor's Degrees. Bachelor's degrees are conferred on graduates who have fulfilled all the requirements of the teaching program and have been approved for graduation. Their coursework achievement and the grade on their graduation thesis, design, or other form of graduation practice must indicate that they have acquired a fairly good command of the basic theories, specialized knowledge, and basic skills in the branch of learning concerned, and that they have shown an ability to undertake scientific research or to engage in technical work.

Institutions of higher education authorized to confer the bachelor's degree evaluate the results of each graduate's studies and examine his or her graduation appraisals through the various departments in charge. Qualified students then are recommended to the Academic Degree Evaluation Committee of their institution for conferral of a bachelor's degree.

Undergraduates who have completed bachelor-degree-level courses of study in non-degree-conferring institutions may be recommended by their department to a degree-conferring institution. The related department in the degree-conferring institution may examine the student and, if he or she meets all requirements, confer a bachelor's degree.

Master's Degrees. Applicants for master's degrees submit an application, thesis, and other material to an academic-degree-conferring unit during the time prescribed by that unit. The unit examines the application within two months, accepts or rejects it, and notifies the applicant and his or her unit of the result. Graduates from non-degree-conferring units submit a letter of recommendation from their own unit to support the application. Applicants with equivalent qualifications must submit two letters of recommendation from associate professors, full professors, or specialists with corresponding titles. A degree conferring unit may choose to examine an applicant without graduate status on some university courses before accepting the application.

Requirements for a master's degree include three to four courses on basic theories and specialized subjects in the branch of learning concerned, reading and research facility in one foreign language, and courses on fundamental Marxist theory.

Each degree-conferring unit arranges to administer examinations for the required courses. Applicants for master's degrees must pass these examinations before they are permitted to take the oral examination on their thesis. In the event of failure, a makeup examination may be taken within six months. Applicants who fail the makeup examination are not allowed to take the oral examination on their master's degree thesis.

Master's degree theses should contain some new ideas about the subject matter to indicate that the author has the ability to undertake scientific research or engage in independent technical work. One or two specialists in the branch of learning concerned read and appraise the thesis. They then make detailed comments on the thesis for the reference of the oral examination board. The oral examination board includes three to five members, including specialists from other units. After the examination, the oral examination board decides by secret ballot whether or not to confer the master's degree; a two-thirds majority of all board members is required. The decision then is submitted to the Academic Degree Evaluation Committee. An applicant who fails the oral examination of the thesis may, with the consent of the oral examination board, revise the thesis and take another oral examination within one year. If a majority of the board believes the applicant's thesis has reached the academic level of the doctoral degree, they, in addition to deciding to confer a master's degree, may propose to a doctoral-degree-conferring unit that the applicant be reviewed for possible conferral of a doctoral degree.

Doctoral Degrees. Applicants for doctoral degrees submit their applications, dissertations, and other materials to a degree-conferring unit during the time established by that unit. The unit examines these within two months of the application deadline, decides whether or not to accept the application, and notifies the applicant and his or her unit of the result. Applicants with equivalent qualifications must submit letters of recommendations from two professors or specialists with a corresponding title. In the case of applicants without a master's degree, a degree-conferring unit may, before accepting the applications, arrange examinations on some of the relevant courses taken.

Requirements for a doctoral degree include the following:

1. A comprehensive grasp of basic theories and specialized knowledge in the branch of learning concerned. The range of examinations is decided by the Academic Degree Evaluation Committee of the degree-conferring unit. Examinations on basic theories and specialized knowledge are conducted by an examination committee composed of three specialists appointed by the Academic Degree Evaluation Committee.
2. Reading, research, and writing facility in one foreign language; reading and research facility in a second foreign language. For applicants in certain fields or specialities, only the first foreign language is required with the approval of the Academic Degree Evaluation Committee of the degree-conferring unit.
3. Courses on Marxist theory at a more advanced level.

Applicants for doctoral degrees must pass the required examinations before they are permitted to take the oral examination on the dissertation. Applicants who have published important works, made discoveries in science and technology, or have contributed to these may submit their publications, appraisals, or certificates of inventions or discoveries to a degree-conferring unit. Upon recommendation by two professors or specialists with a corresponding title, the unit may examine and approve these materials and exempt the applicant from part or all of the course examinations.

Dissertations must indicate that the author has the ability to undertake independent scientific research and has made creative achievements in science or technology. Dissertations, or their abstracts, are sent to related units three months prior to the oral examination on the dissertation for review and appraisial by two specialists in the branch of learning concerned; one of these specialists must be from another unit. The specialists make detailed comments on the dissertation from the reference of the oral examination board.

The oral examination board is composed of five to seven members, the majority of whom must be professors or specialists with a corresponding title. Two or three members of the board must be from other units. After the oral examination, the board decides by secret ballot whether or not to confer the doctoral degree; a two-thirds majority of the members is required. The decision then is submitted to the Academic Degree Evaluation Committee. Generally, oral examinations are conducted in public. After a dissertation, or its abstract, has been passed, it is published.

If the oral examination board believes that the applicant's dissertation does not attain the academic level of a doctoral degree but does reach that of a master's degree, the board may decide to confer a master's degree on the applicant if he or she has not yet received that degree in the subject concerned.

Honorary Doctoral Degrees. The conferral of honorary doctoral degrees must be approved by the Academic Degree Evaluation Committee of degree-conferring units, which submit the recommendation to the Academic Degree Committee of the State Council for approval.

Other Stipulations. Foreign students who are studying in China and foreign scholars who are teaching or engaged in research work in China who wish to apply for a bachelor's, master's, or doctoral degree are treated according to the same regulations as are Chinese students and scholars.

The form of the certificate for the bachelor's degree is designed by the State Education Commission. Those for the master's degree and the doctoral degree are designed by the Academic Degree Committee of the State Council.

One copy of approved theses for master's degrees and of dissertations for doctoral degrees is kept in the library of the degree-conferring unit. One copy of approved dissertations for doctoral degrees is also kept in the National Library of China and in other related specialized libraries.

Individuals applying for a master's degree or a doctoral degree, after being approved by a degree-conferring-unit to take the course examinations and the oral examination on the thesis or dissertation, may be granted a leave of not more than two months to prepare for the examinations.

Degree-conferring units may establish additional stipulations on conferring academic degrees, using the Regulations Concerning Academic Degrees in the People's Republic of China as a basis.

Higher Education Self-Study Examinations

Higher Education Self-Study Examination Guidance Committees administer state examinations to self-taught students. These committees are directly under the jurisdiction of the central government, with state authorization. Depending on demand and the ability to undertake such examinations, the committees decide what subjects are to be examined and arrange examination plans and course outlines accordingly. Higher education self-study examinations are divided into three categories: regular college courses, specialized courses, and basic courses. Examinations for different courses are conducted separately. Individuals who have acquired a sufficient number of credits are entitled to receive graduation certificates for specialized/basic courses or regular college courses. Their school records are recognized by the state, and they are considered equivalent to graduates from regular institutions of higher education.

The higher education self-study examination system has been spreading gradually throughout China. Self-study examination guidance committees have now been established in all 29 provinces, autonomous regions, and municipalities on mainland China. Examinations have been conducted in 148 specialized subjects in liberal arts, science and engineering, agronomy, finance and economics, and political science and law. Nearly one million individuals throughout the country have registered for such examinations. Over the past few years, 1,169,012 certificates of qualification for individual courses have been issued throughout China. In Beijing, Tianjin, Shanghai, and Liaoning, where initial experiments with self-study examinations were conducted, 1,582 individuals have received graduate certificates for specialized college courses.

The higher education self-study examinations in China are conducted on two levels, central and local. The National Higher Education Self-Study Examination Guidance Committee is responsible for the formulation of policies and guiding principles concerning the examinations, including the selection of specialized courses for examination, standard examination criteria, and operating instructions for the examination itself. There are 11 specialized subcommittees of the national committee, composed of experts and professors, whose tasks are to map out national plans for specialized course examinations and curricular examination programs and to organize the compilation and selection of teaching materials and guidebooks that meet the needs of individuals who study by themselves. The Higher Education Self-Study Examination Guidance Committees in various provinces, autonomous regions, and municipalities are responsible for the organization of local self-study examinations, the designation of the colleges or schools that administer the examinations, the assignment of examination papers, the grading of such papers, and other matters.

A number of opportunities are available to assist individuals who wish to study on their own, including guidance classes attached to colleges; continuation schools run by social organizations, democratic parties, or individuals; advisory centers established by government organizations or industrial and mining enterprises; lectures on radio and television; and helpful columns in newspapers and periodicals.

Summary

The policies and procedures adopted after the death of Mao and subsequent downfall of the "Gang of Four" are designed to ensure that only the most academically qualified students gain admission to China's colleges and universities. Academic achievement, as measured by uniform national examinations in most cases, is clearly the most important factor in the enrollment process; however, physical health and, occasionally, a personal interview also play a role. Family background may also be a factor in selection decisions. There is no question as to the high quality of those admitted to the most prestigious institutions; given the large size of the applicant pool and the importance of academic qualification, it would be surprising if the postsecondary-level student population were other than "the best and the brightest."

Having noted the high caliber of university students, it is important to call attention to a number of other features of the current selection procedures. For example, it seems highly likely that most—probably an overwhelming majority of—postsecondary level students come from urban or suburban areas. The poorer quality of secondary schools in most rural areas all but precludes successful competition in the national examinations. Moreover, home environment gives an edge to the children of intellectuals, officials, and certain kinds of skilled workers. This advantage is perpetuated, even exaggerated, by the system of key primary and secondary schools. Given China's needs and the logic of the current strategy of development, this is considered a necessary and proper situation. A major concern, though, is to expand alternative opportunities fast enough to satisfy those disadvantaged by present policies.

Another noteworthy characteristic of current enrollment policies is that the next generation of intellectuals will have formal ties to the Communist Party. Official reports indicate that 70 to 85 percent of those enrolled in institutions of higher education in the early 1980s belonged to either the party or the Communist Youth League. Clearly the relationship between the party and those with badly needed skills will be different than in the past.

Once admitted to one of the 1,063 institutions of higher education, students are trained in narrow specialities offering few opportunities for cross or extradisciplinary work. Some academicians in China have begun to call for changes in this area, but change, when it does comes, is likely to be very gradual.

PART TWO

Educational Exchanges: An Overview

China's experience with educational exchanges has been substantially different from that of the United States. Whereas China has sent large numbers of students abroad for training—to Japan and the United States before World War II, to the Soviet Union and Eastern Europe during the 1950s and early 1960s, and to the West and Japan since 1977—the United States, especially since 1945, has received far more students and scholars than it has sent abroad. Although many more U.S. than Chinese students study abroad, most of the Americans attend overseas branches of their home institutions or participate in special one- or two-semester programs on foreign campuses. In contrast, Chinese students who go abroad generally spend several years at foreign universities. Most Americans who study abroad are undergraduates; most Chinese are graduate students. China has received far fewer students than it has sent abroad; indeed, several U.S. universities have on campus as many foreign students as there are in all of China.

The list of contrasts can easily be extended; the point is not simply that the two countries have had different experiences, but that they approach educational exchanges with different objectives and expectations.

7
China's Approach to Educational Exchanges

The Chinese government began sending students abroad more than a century ago, but the Qing dynasty and its two successors, the Republic of China and the People's Republic of China, displayed considerable ambivalence about the value of such an effort. On the one hand, successive governments have viewed exchanges as an effective way to acquire the knowledge and technical skills needed to modernize China. On the other hand, they have recognized the perils of sending their brightest students to live in countries with very different political systems and standards of living. Consistent with this ambivalence, the pattern of Chinese students going abroad is one of recurring peaks and valleys. During the 1950s and early 1960s, China's new government sent approximately 40,000 students to the Soviet Union and Eastern Europe to study subjects ranging from aerodynamics to zoology. The objective of this program was to acquire badly needed skills and familiarity with all aspects of the Soviet model of development. Chinese and Soviet officials attached high priority to this program; despite inevitable defects, it was remarkably effective.

The flow of Chinese students going abroad dwindled to a mere trickle in the early 1960s because of the political rift with Moscow and the isolationism of the Cultural Revolution. The number of Chinese studying in other countries increased in the late 1960s, but the total was small, consisting almost entirely of equal exchanges between China and other Third World countries. China and her exchange partners certainly benefited from this exchange, but few Chinese participants acquired the kind of advanced training characteristic of earlier exchanges with the Soviet Union.

Reviewing the history of the Cultural Revolution, Chinese leaders concluded, probably as early as 1972, that rapid and sustained modernization of the country was impossible without extensive contacts between scholars in China and the advanced industrial states. The domestic political situation precluded major restructuring of exchange programs until after the death of Mao Zedong and the purge of the

"Gang of Four" in 1976. Once such obstacles were removed, the new leadership acted with dispatch to open new avenues for study abroad. Since 1978, sending students and scholars abroad to earn degrees and conduct research has been an integral part of China's policy to upgrade its educational system and obtain the professional manpower necessary to meet the goals of modernization. Large numbers of Chinese students and scholars have been sent to Western Europe, Japan, and the United States for training that complemented China's developmental strategy emphasizing science and technology.

As exchanges have developed since 1978, various components of the Chinese education sector have become involved in exchange programs. It is clear that individual institutions and faculty/students in China have their own objectives and expectations, and it is important to distinguish among different groups or interests. Those interests cannot be discussed in great detail here, but the following broad outline may be helpful.

Government officials responsible for coordination of science and education seek to identify and prepare the best possible candidates for study abroad with an eye to overall national needs. As a result, they have given priority to students in certain scientific and engineering disciplines rather than to those in other fields. They hope to place as many officially sponsored students as possible in first-rate foreign programs; China's best should be in the best available programs. One consequence of this policy is a sense of competition between government-sponsored candidates and those with private sponsorship (e.g., from relatives or friends outside China, or from an institution or department to which a student has applied independently). Although Chinese officials recognize the advantages of having as many students as possible studying abroad, they seem to prefer having foreign institutions give preference to government-sponsored students who are studying subjects particularly relevant to meeting national objectives.

Individual Chinese colleges and universities have objectives that are sometimes different from those of officials in Beijing. More specifically, they may be more interested in placing their own students and faculty in good foreign programs than in following a national plan. They are in competition with one another as well as with the State Education Commission; since not all Chinese applicants can be accepted, they would prefer that those who are accepted come from their own institution.

Chinese organizations—from the State Education Commission, Chinese Academy of Sciences, and Chinese Academy of Social Sciences to individual institutions—seem to prefer orderly and predictable exchange arrangements. For example, they want to know who is responsible for making arrangements in China and the United States (e.g., who will assist Chinese students on a particular U.S. campus and who is responsible for Americans studying or conducting research in China). Because of competition for slots and limited foreign exchange, they favor institution-to-institution ties (often called "sister institution agreements" by the Chinese) that guarantee a certain number of study opportunities in particular schools or departments. At the same time, however, they welcome the flexibility of U.S. higher education that allows them to take advantage of multiple channels of access, to seek acceptance and funding through a variety of ways, and to avoid the drawbacks of quotas or central placement mechanisms. There is a healthy self-confidence behind this attitude that assumes Chinese candidates will be able to compete effectively with other applicants. This confidence may be well founded, given the intense competition within China. Still, they would like assurance that a minimum number of people will have opportunities to study abroad even if they are not yet competitive; hence the desire for assured slots in partner institutions.

China's current plan for sending students and scholars abroad is outlined in the Seventh Five-Year Plan (1986–90), which is briefly described below.

1. The number of individuals to be sent abroad at government expense will remain approximately the same as the 1985–86 level (slightly fewer than 5,000 students and scholars), but the overall number of persons going abroad for educational purposes will increase as a large proportion of slots for graduate students are allocated to various localities, departments, and institutions, which will pay for the exchanges from their own funds.

2. The emphasis on study or research abroad will be on disciplines needed for the modernization of China. Specific disciplines will be determined by local units funding students and scholars, depending on their individual needs. The funding units will enter into an agreement with the individuals they are sending abroad so that a specific subject will be studied.

3. The number of students studying for a master's degree abroad will be reduced; the number of students studying for a doctoral degree abroad will be increased. Once an individual has received a Ph.D. abroad, he or she must return to China to work for a certain period of time before going abroad again to assure continued study or research will be geared to China's needs. Special funds will be allocated for doctoral degree holders to continue exchanges with foreign experts and possibly travel abroad to participate in academic conferences or

conduct postdoctoral research.

4. The highest caliber of students and scholars will continue to be sent abroad.

5. Regarding self-sponsored students: greater efforts will be made to "guide and control them so that their selection will conform with state requirements, will meet certain goals, and will be carried out in a planned way."

Just as there are varied attitudes toward the sending of students and scholars abroad, so, too, are there many different opinions about receiving foreigners in China. Although the State Education Commission and other national organizations in China have more authority and greater capacity to make things happen than does the U.S. Department of Education, the burden of hosting foreigners falls not on those agencies but on individual institutions, departments, and faculty. The national government can agree in the abstract to facilitate certain types of projects in China, but their ultimate success depends on resources further along in the system. Unfortunately, those resources are stretched very thinly, and accommodating students and researchers can be a heavy burden for the host organization.

8

The U.S. Approach to Exchanges with China

As in China, there are many different attitudes in the United States toward U.S.-China educational exchanges. Although the federal government negotiated the umbrella agreement opening the way for educational exchanges, Washington does not have the ability to place applicants from China. (In the October 1978 U.S.-China meetings, the Chinese team rejected the U.S. government's offer to help establish, but not operate, centralized placement services.) The burden of actually conducting educational exchanges falls primarily on the nation's colleges and universities. Within the academic community, willingness to establish exchange relationships with China generally has been quite high. Some of the leading research universities in the United States have been among the first and most active exchange partners of Chinese institutions.

Initially, many institutions—or individuals within them—were eager to receive their first students or scholars from the PRC. Faculty members, including Chinese-American faculty, were curious about the work being done by colleagues in Chinese institutions. Schools with programs in China studies were eager to enable their students and faculty to study or conduct research in China; others were swept along by the "China fever" of 1979–80.

The general institutional and individual willingness to take whatever unorthodox measures were necessary to initiate exchanges with China have been tempered by conviction that extraordinary measures could only be temporary. The overall objective was to place exchanges with China on the same footing as those with other countries as soon as possible. Chinese students should compete with other applicants seeking admission and financial aid, and decisions should be based on normal or consistent criteria. This did not always happen in the first years after the resumption of the exchanges, but has become much more common in recent years.

Many U.S. institutions appear more interested in receiving students from China than in sending their own students to the PRC. This results in part from awareness that few postsecondary-level programs in China are appropriate for their students and that few U.S. students have the language skills needed to participate in the programs in any case. Few U.S. institutions or individuals seem troubled by the disparity in numbers; they are, however, becoming increasingly concerned about differences in access to libraries, archives, and field research in specific cases. At the risk of overgeneralizing, it seems fair to say that the common attitude is that U.S. institutions and departments have done everything possible to help students and scholars from China attain their study objectives in the United States. They believe it is appropriate, therefore, for China to do all she can to accommodate the wishes and needs of those U.S. students and faculty who want to work in the PRC. While some progress has been made in this area, problems persist.

American attitudes toward exchanges in general and with China in particular are also shaped by concern that willingness to receive large numbers of foreign students, especially in graduate programs involving highly sensitive research in science and engineering, contributes to the partial or perceived loss of U.S. dominance in certain technical fields. This concern is often directed more at students from technologically advanced countries, such as Japan, West Germany, and France, than at students from developing countries, but it raises questions about the wisdom of exchanges that inevitably affects all countries. A related concern involves the gap between the actual cost of educating students in the United States and the portion of that cost recovered through tuition and fees. Since this gap is large and growing, especially in fields requiring expensive equipment, questions have been raised about the propriety and wisdom of using institutional or government resources to subsidize large numbers of foreign students. This relatively recent concern is being voiced at a time when educational exchanges with China are growing, at an increasing cost to U.S. institutions. Finally, attitudes toward exchanges with China have been affected in part by previous experiences with the Soviet Union and Eastern Europe. China's willingness to send large numbers of students and scholars abroad, and to accommodate numerous U.S. students and scholars, has been contrasted with the more restrictive exchanges with other Communist countries. At the U.S. national level, this has led to broad encouragement and some financial support for exchanges with China.

9

U.S.-Chinese Agreements Governing the Exchange of Students and Scholars

Educational exchanges between the United States and China have developed without elaborate government-to-government agreements. As a direct result of the July 1978 visit to China by President Carter's science adviser, Frank Press, the basic document authorizing and encouraging such exchanges was concluded in October 1978, two months before Washington and Beijing announced that diplomatic relations would be normalized on January 1, 1979. Although both sides anticipated normalization, the agreement entitled "Understanding on the Exchange of Students and Scholars Between the United States of America and the People's Republic of China" was not predicated on the establishment of diplomatic relations. It was, however, an important agreement, for it signalled willingness by the United States to assist China's drive for rapid modernization and willingness by China to enter into an entirely different relationship with the United States.

The Understanding was later subsumed under the umbrella "Agreement on Cooperation in Science and Technology" signed by President Carter and Vice Premier Deng Xiaoping on January 31, 1979. (The Agreement is reproduced in Appendix A.) As a result, educational exchanges fall within the purview of the U.S.-PRC Joint Commission on Scientific and Technological Cooperation, which meets annually to review programs. Ironically, colleges and universities do not have formal representation on the U.S. side of the commission. The Agreement was extended for another five years in January 1984 when Premier Zhao Ziyang visited Washington.

On July 23, 1985, Li Xiannian, president of the People's Republic of China, and President Reagan signed a "Protocol for Cooperation in Educational Exchanges" between the United States and China, as well as an implementing accord for cultural exchanges in 1986 and 1987 under the cultural agreement between the United States and China. The educational protocol supersedes the "Understanding on the

Exchange of Students between the United States of America and the People's Republic of China" signed in October 1978. The principal objective of the accord is to provide opportunities for cooperation and exchange in educational fields based on equality, reciprocity, and mutual benefit. Both countries will initiate educational exchange activities based on their own as well as mutual interests, and will to every extent possible assure that the requests of the sending side for necessary study and research opportunities are met in accordance with each country's laws and regulations. The principles of the accord will be the basis of all official educational exchanges; non-official arrangements, to the degree applicable, should also follow these principles. (The Protocol is reproduced in Appendix B.)

The contents of the Protocol were confirmed in discussions held between He Dongchang, vice chairman of the State Education Commission of China, and Marvin L. Stone, acting director of the U.S. Information Agency, on June 3, 1987. During the meeting, He Dongchang outlined China's policy on sending students abroad. He said that foreign study for Chinese students is part of the Chinese government's policy of opening to the outside world, to which China will continue to adhere. He said that sending students abroad must serve the domestic development of the People's Republic of China, and that sponsored personnel studying abroad are sent according to plans to meet the development needs of the region, department, or unit from which they come. Therefore, there are unequivocal stipulations concerning the fields and length of study of all sponsored students and scholars. In view of the recent rapid development of graduate education in China, Vice Chairman He said China will increasingly concentrate on sending sponsored students and scholars who have already obtained their master's or doctoral degrees and senior scholars who possess extensive experience working in educational or scientific research and development at Chinese universities or scientific institutions.

10

Students and Scholars from China in the United States

Several studies have been conducted on Chinese students and scholars in the United States since the resumption of educational exchanges between the United States and China. The first comprehensive survey, completed by the U.S.-China Education Clearinghouse in 1981, resulted in the publication *Students and Scholars from the People's Republic of China in the United States, August 1981: A Survey Summary* . This was followed by a survey and publication produced by the National Academy Press in 1986, *A Relationship Restored: Trends in U.S.-China Educational Exchanges, 1978–1984*. A new publication produced by the National Academy Press, *Chinese Students in America: Policies, Issues, and Numbers*, provides more up-to-date information.

According to the most recent publication, the U.S Embassy and consulates in China issued just under 50,000 visas to students and scholars from 1979 through 1986. Almost two-thirds of these were J-1 visas, which were fairly evenly divided between students and scholars. Engineering and science remain the dominant, though diminishing, fields of specialization for students and scholars on J-1 visas. A much higher proportion of students on F-1 visas are enrolled in the fields of social sciences and humanities. In 1985, women constituted 20 percent of students on J-1 visas, and 41 percent of students on F-1 visas.

Both students and scholars are younger now than when exchanges began, but the majority still are coming from large urban centers of coastal provinces. Upon arrival in the United States, they are dispersed relatively uniformly across much of the United States, although there are concentrations in New York and California (as has been the case since exchanges resumed).

There have been great changes in the source of financial support of Chinese students and scholars in the United States. In 1979, 57 percent of students on J-1 visas were supported by the Chinese government. In contrast, in 1985 U.S. institutions provided support to 64 percent of students on J-1 visas, with the Chinese government and work units providing support to only 14 percent. Research conducted recently by U.S. Embassy personnel in Beijing indicates that U.S. colleges and universities are by far the major source of financial aid for Chinese applicants, with Chinese government sources second.

As China's institutions have improved, expanded, and established graduate departments, the emphasis has shifted to sending scholars and advanced graduate students abroad, especially at the doctoral and postdoctoral levels. The Chinese are projecting that by 1990 there will be between 7,000 and 8,000 Chinese-trained Ph.D. holders who will go abroad to pursue research.

The number of Chinese students and scholars in the United States continues to increase rapidly, from approximately 3,500 in the academic years between 1978 and 1981 to more than 25,000 in the 1987–88 academic year. According to *Open Doors: 1987/88*, published by the Institute of International Education, there were 25,168 Chinese students in the United States in the 1987–88 academic year (a 26 percent increase over the 1986–87 academic year), 75 percent at the graduate level, 20 percent at the undergraduate level, and 5 percent pursuing other studies. (The *Open Doors* survey does not include scholars.) In November 1986, the Embassy of the People's Republic of China provided the following statistics for students and scholars who were in the United States on J-1 visas for a period of longer than six months: 4,987 scholars (46 percent), 5,716 graduate students (53 percent), and 116 undergraduate students (one percent), totaling 10,819.

To assist the increasing number of Chinese students and scholars applying to U.S. colleges and universities each year, the Chinese and U.S. governments are attempting to provide needed materials and training. Some of the problems initially experienced when U.S.-China educational exchanges recommenced in 1979, such as lack of knowledge of each other's educational system, different definitions of subject matter, courses, and fields, unfamiliarity with governmental regulations and procedures, language difficulties, and cultural differences, have been ameliorated with experience. Notable achievements have occurred during the last nine years:

1. Some U.S. standardized admissions examinations—the Graduate Record Examination, Graduate Management Admission Test, Test of English as a Foreign Language, and Test of Spoken English—now are administered in China, although the demand for them is greater than the availability.

2. English-language training in China has improved, and more students who wish to receive training are able to do so.

3. Educational advising centers have been established to assist stu-

dents and scholars who wish to come to the United States. However, many of these centers are not staffed by trained personnel—or by anyone at all. Some libraries where materials about the U.S. higher education system are maintained have no staff to explain the materials or make certain they are readily available.

4. Information about U.S. institutions of higher education, procedures about applying for admission, requirements for admission (financial, language, and academic), procedures for obtaining appropriate U.S. visas, information about life in the United States, and many other important aspects of the exchange process are becoming somewhat more available.

The State Education Commission of China and the U.S. Information Agency (USIA) currently are working to enhance the educational advising centers that have been established in China (see Appendix C). USIA has sent several international educational specialists to the advising centers in China to conduct training workshops for the personnel. In 1988–89, a foreign-student-admissions specialist, funded by the U.S. government, will provide advice, guidance, and support to the advising centers on a continuing basis. The State Education Commission also sent one if its employees to be trained in the United States in 1987–88; he will return to China in the fall of 1988 to begin working directly with the advising centers.

In addition to the eight educational advising centers for which the State Education Commission is responsible, a ninth center is jointly administered by the Institute of International Education and Guangdong Province. Called the Guangdong American Study Information Center, it opened in October 1985 in Guangzhou and has attracted clients from the Guangzhou area and other provinces.

A relatively new association, the Chinese Educational Association for International Exchanges (CEAIE), is attempting to assist privately sponsored students to identify appropriate U.S. institutions to which to apply. The association is essentially private. Although some funding currently is received from the State Education Commission, each of its five branches is mainly supported by the institutions of higher education in the city in which the branch is located. The Shanghai Branch of the CEAIE, for example, has a membership of 31 institutions.

In summary, by whatever means Chinese students and scholars learn about and find ways to attend institutions of higher education in the United States, it is obvious that there is a highly selective process in China to assure that talented people are sent to the United States. Once they are here, they perform extremely well academically.

11

U.S. Students, Researchers, and Teachers in China

A large imbalance exists in the flow of students and scholars between China and the United States, similar to disparities that exist between the United States and all developing countries. There simply are more reasons and opportunities to study in the United States. According to statistics provided to NAFSA by the State Education Commission in October 1987, 35,000 Chinese students and scholars had been to the United States between 1979 and 1986 (8,000 of whom had returned to China). Some 6,600 U.S. students had been to China, and 4,000 Americans had taught in China.

The experiences of U.S. students, researchers, and teachers in China have been extremely diverse. Although situations have at times been frustrating, the majority of new "China hands" agree they were able to learn a great deal about China and its people, and about themselves, while in the PRC, and were very glad to have had the opportunity to share everyday life in China. (Details of these experiences, and information for others planning extended stays in China, appear in *China Bound: A Guide to Academic Life and Work in the PRC*, published by the National Academy Press.)

12

U.S.-China Educational Exchanges in a Global Context

Although it is difficult to obtain complete statistics about international educational exchanges, the Chinese government estimates that between January 1978 and mid-1987, 50,000 Chinese students and scholars had been sent to approximately 70 countries, 40,000 officially sponsored and 10,000 privately financed. Of that total, approximately 20,000 have completed their studies and research and returned to China.

In 1985, the State Education Commission sent 4,808 students and scholars abroad under government sponsorship, including 1,902 to the United States, 562 to Japan, 479 to the United Kingdom, 420 to Germany, 346 to France, 331 to Canada, 217 to the Soviet Union and Eastern European countries, 190 to Asian countries other than Japan, 147 to Norway, Sweden, Denmark, and Finland, 92 to Switzerland, the Netherlands, and Belgium, 44 to Italy and Balkan and Iberian countries, 42 to African nations, and 36 to Latin American countries. In addition to students and scholars, 721 Chinese college and university teachers went to 29 countries from 1979 through mid-1985, mainly in the fields of foreign languages, literature, and history.

In the reverse, 2,498 foreign students from 80 countries studied on a long-term basis at Chinese institutions of higher education from 1973 to 1978; 948 (38 percent) were from developing countries. From 1979 to 1985, 6,541 foreign students from 109 countries studied on a long-term basis at Chinese institutions of higher education; 4,141 (63 percent) were from industrialized countries. In the 1985–86 academic year, there were 3,251 long-term foreign students in China; 1,842 (57 percent) were from Third World countries. In addition, 12,951 foreign students enrolled in short-term courses at Chinese institutions of higher education between 1978 and 1984. One-fourth of the long-term students received scholarships from the Chinese government; all short-term students were self-supporting.

Between 1953 and 1962, 862 foreign experts were teaching in China. Of these, 761 were from the Soviet Union, the rest from Eastern

European and Asian socialist countries. These experts played a significant role in developing Chinese higher education, exerting an
immense influence on the structure, curricula, staff development, and
other aspects of the academic life of Chinese institutions of higher
education. Between 1978 and mid-1985, 721 foreign experts went to
China on a long-term basis and 4,344 as short-term lecturers. In the
1984–85 academic year, foreign experts from 26 different countries
were in China. In the 1985–86 academic year, there were 1,479 foreign
experts in China. Most (1,289) were language teachers (English—854,
Japanese—153, French—75, German—80, other—127), 82 were in scientific and technical fields, and 108 in humanities and social sciences.

By December 1987, 400 Chinese institutions of higher education
had established partnerships with 700 U.S. institutions. Between July
1982 and June 1985, the 36 colleges and universities under the authority of the State Education Commission established partnership relations with 320 foreign institutions. These partnerships have been
particularly effective in promoting the exchange of students and scholars, arranging the exchange of visiting groups and delegations, conducting joint research projects, providing short-term training courses,
and exchanging publications and information.

While these exchanges have benefited China in numerous ways,
they also have raised concerns. Chinese government officials are not so
much worried about the influences the returning Chinese students
and scholars might have on Chinese society, as they are whether the
students and scholars actually will return, and how their newly
acquired expertise can be utilized properly. Individuals returning
from experiences overseas have tended to advance more rapidly
within administrative and research establishments, but there are difficulties. Chinese government officials are trying to improve the job-
assignment process; they also are attempting to make certain that
students and scholars who go abroad learn the skills that are most
needed and important to the development of the country. They are
concerned about the ability of China to effectively absorb and utilize
huge numbers of new graduate-degree holders from Chinese institutions as well as from abroad. Chinese authorities readily confess to a
surfeit of certain types of doctorates and a desperate shortage of others.

Considerable concern is expressed over the return issue. In March
1988, several Western newspapers reported that Chinese government
officials were advocating a drastic reduction in the number of students
sent abroad, particularly to the United States, because of a "growing
concern in Beijing that too many young scholars may stay overseas or
become too Westernized" (*New York Times*). Chinese government representatives and U.S. government officials in Beijing have repudiated

this report. The official government statement, issued in Beijing on April 5, 1988, by Huang Xinbai (who is in charge of study abroad activities for the State Education Commission of China), maintained that "sending students to study abroad is China's longstanding policy which remains unchanged and will never change." He further commented that the reports in the Western press were ". . . groundless. . . based on hearsay and. . . fabricated with ulterior motives." With the approval of the State Council, Huang said, the State Education Commission publicized a regulation entitled "Some Temporary Provisions for Sending People to Study Abroad" on June 11, 1987. "There is no change in the principles set forth in the regulation," he reported.

Detailed stipulations of the June 11, 1987 regulation are provided in other sections of this publication. However, the overall principle of the regulation follows:

> China has accomplished a great deal in the work of sending people to study abroad through different channels. This is in complete accord with China's long-term policy of opening to the world and will be continued unswervingly. . . . the policy of expanding all avenues of study abroad in accordance with the needs of the construction of socialist material and spiritual civilization shall be adhered to for a long time to come.

Huang indicated that there are three means for students to go abroad to study: through government channels, with the help of the institution or department in which the student works, and through self-sponsorship. In 1987, approximately 3,000 students were sent abroad through government channels, 4,000 by institutions or departments, and 2,000 on self-sponsorship. Yu Fuzeng, director of the Foreign Affairs Bureau of the State Education Commission, told U.S. Embassy personnel in April 1988 to expect no significant changes in these numbers in the near future. He anticipates that the State Education Commission will send approximately 600 students per year to pursue higher education in the United States (20 percent of the total number of students sent abroad by the State Education Commission annually); and that local, municipal, and provincial organizations will send another 3,000 to 4,000 officially sponsored students per year to the United States. He indicated there have been no recent changes in regulations or procedures to restrict self-sponsored students and anticipated none in the future. Yu also mentioned that, to improve the State Education Commission's records of officially sponsored students sent abroad, the commission has devised a form modeled on the U.S. Form

IAP-66, and is requesting that provincial, municipal, and local government organizations complete and submit this form for each student sent overseas.

Because of the need to better manage the system of sending students abroad and to ensure that what they learn can be applied to internal development, some adjustments are being made in the policy for state-funded students studying abroad. These include the following:

- Subject matter: students will be encouraged to major in applied fields of study.
- Categories of students sent abroad: since China has become more capable in training undergraduate and graduate students, students will generally not be sent abroad to study at the undergraduate level, and the number of students studying abroad for master's degrees will be reduced. At the same time, more individuals will be sent abroad to pursue advanced studies and serve as visiting scholars, including those who have received a Ph.D. degree in China or abroad.
- Choice of country: based on China's needs, more students will be sent to countries capable of accepting an increased number of Chinese students but which have taken very few so far.

New restrictions on the time allowed to attain degrees in the United States were publicly announced in November 1987, based upon the State Education Commission's better understanding of the U.S. educational system. The following limits have been set on the time allowed for officially sponsored Chinese students to attain their graduate degrees in the United States: up to three years for a master's degree, a base of up to five years for a doctoral degree (with an exceptional extension for an additional year possible in unusual cases), and an occasional permission for up to 18 months of postgraduate research following a five-year Ph.D.

It thus appears that enforcement of regulations regarding overseas study, which have been in effect for some time, is becoming more diligent. Also, as noted earlier, individual work units have been granted more authority to make decisions about who will be granted permission to study abroad, in what subject areas, and for what periods of time.

PART THREE

The Exchange Process: Regulations and Procedures

The first Chinese students and scholars who came to the United States in 1979 were concentrated at relatively few well-known U.S. institutions. As more information about the U.S. education system and the variety of U.S. institutions of higher education has become available in China, Chinese citizens have applied to a much larger number of U.S. institutions. The U.S. government has placed collections of general reference materials about U.S. higher education in nine educational advising centers and 23 libraries throughout China, and has requested that all interested U.S. institutions send their catalogs to be included in these collections. (Lists of collection locations and contents appear in Appendix C.) Since the U.S. Embassy in Beijing has not subscribed to the catalog distribution service of the U.S. Information Agency, through which U.S. institutions can have their catalogs mailed to posts around the world, institutional catalogs should be sent directly (via air mail) to the sites listed in Appendix C.

Educational exchanges between the United States and China have become easier and more fruitful as more has been learned about possibilities and procedures in each country. Part Three addresses questions that have been posed by U.S. college and university personnel working with Chinese students and scholars. Readers must proceed with caution, however. Although regulations and procedures affecting international educational exchanges in China have stabilized since exchanges with the United States were resumed, and the overall policy of study abroad has recently been reaffirmed, changes still do occur. Information about future changes will be made available through NAFSA's periodicals as they occur.

13
Admissions Information

In addition to the usual problems encountered in interpreting academic credentials from other countries, special difficulties exist with respect to China. Lack of communication between the United States and China for nearly 30 years precluded familiarity with each other's academic customs. Furthermore, the Cultural Revolution disrupted recordkeeping in China and created wide disparities between the academic preparation and career patterns of individual Chinese. Many of the problems are diminishing as U.S. foreign student admissions personnel gain familiarity with China's education system and institutions, and as more Chinese applicants receive their training in the education system instituted after the end of the Cultural Revolution. However, difficulties still exist, especially due to changes in institutional names and the opening of new institutions about which no information is available. In such instances, admissions officers are encouraged to write to the Chinese institution to request information about its founding, course offerings, etc., and to share this information with colleagues through the *NAFSA Newsletter*.

U.S. institutions are encouraged to follow normal admissions or invitation procedures as closely as possible when dealing with applications or requests from students or scholars in the PRC. Chinese applicants can submit copies of official documents with the government seal, scores from the Chinese National College Entrance Examinations, detailed descriptions of courses taken, and information about levels of English from their teachers. Some U.S. standardized admissions tests also are administered in China (see below). However, there are still many questions about various educational institutions in China, and U.S. institutions may have to determine the exact placement of Chinese students after their arrival. A student may therefore not be accorded degree-seeking status until a semester's work and test results are available for review.

An overall review of the structure of the Chinese educational system, the organization and types of institutions of higher education in China, and selection procedures and academic programs is provided in the first part of this publication. Additional information to help admissions officers assess academic credentials from China is given below.

Colleges and Universites

When the Nationalist government moved to Taiwan in 1949, many educational records went with it. For this reason, some credentials for college work completed in China before 1949 may be certified by educational authorities now on Taiwan.

Some academic records dated in the early 1950s may be confusing because educational institutions were extensively reorganized in 1952–53. As part of this reorganization, names were changed, departments were moved from one institution to another, and some schools ceased to exist entirely. After the reorganization, however, considerable stability existed until the onset of the Cultural Revolution in 1966. Credentials for the 1953–66 period are fairly complete, but many have been lost or destroyed during the turmoil of the Cultural Revolution.

All colleges were closed from 1966 to 1971. Credentials will not be available for this period. Some "degrees" may have been granted for work begun before 1966, but they do not reflect any work done after the spring of 1966.

Students who entered institutions of higher education between the fall of 1971 and the fall of 1976 graduated after usually three, or sometimes two, and in a very few cases four, years. Curricula included a great deal of political study, manual work, and production-oriented training; there was little basic science, and virtually no work in foreign languages. Students were selected by their work units after spending a minimum of two years in "productive labor." The selection process emphasized class origin (worker or peasant families) and political attitude. Little weight was attached to formal academic credentials, and examinations were rarely used. Despite the anti-intellectual attitude that prevailed at the time and the fact that educators and political leaders have denigrated this generation of students, some very bright youth were apparently selected by their peers for college study during this period. Their aptitude and achievements may be difficult to discern in academic records, however.

In assessing applications from the students who studied during 1971–77, admissions officers should be alert to the existence of "uncertified scholars"—dedicated students who studied at home, or worked in research institutes where they were able to benefit from informal training.

The college class selected in the late fall of 1977, which actually entered college in the spring of 1978, completed its studies in the spring of 1982. These students were selected on the basis of college entrance examinations standardized at the provincial rather than the national level. Chinese sources have stated that "recommendation" still played a part in their selection, however, and that some students from other than worker or peasant backgrounds were discouraged from seeking college entrance.

The college system returned to "normal" in the fall of 1978, when students were enrolled directly from senior-middle schools through nationally standardized tests. A four-year curriculum was reinstated, and the first "normal" college class graduated in the spring of 1982. Students who excelled in their studies were awarded a bachelor's degree (see Chapter 6).

Graduate Education

Graduate education, known as "postgraduate study," was begun in China around 1956; by the onset of the Cultural Revolution in 1966, Chinese institutions had trained approximately 16,000 students at the graduate level. Those completing graduate programs received certificates of completion rather than formal degrees. Approximately 3,000 Chinese graduate students studied in the Soviet Union and Eastern Europe between 1955 and the early 1960s. A considerable number of these graduate scholars were "enrolled" at research institutes of the Chinese Academy of Sciences; some of their credentials may have been issued by the academy. It is not known whether any certificates were issued to persons who had only partially completed their graduate work by 1966. In some but by no means all research institutes, work did not come to an abrupt halt in 1966, and graduate work may have been completed in the late 1960s.

No formal graduate education was provided between 1966 and the fall of 1978, when graduate studies were reestablished. At that time, approximately 10,000 students enrolled in over 200 colleges and universities and roughly 150 research institutes. Graduate training consisted primarily of research apprenticeships with senior researchers. Programs were of at least three years' duration in most cases, with 60 credits earned during the first two years and a research paper prepared during the third year. The first new generation of scholars to have completed graduate work would therefore not have been eligible to go abroad until the fall of 1981.

China is placing great emphasis on improving its graduate programs. The first group of higher education institutions was authorized to confer master's and doctoral degrees in 1981 (see Chapter 6).

Some individuals who enroll in U.S. institutions, sometimes in a non-degree status, are mid-career professionals seeking advanced training and practical experience with colleagues in their field of specialization. When accepting "visiting scholars," U.S. institutions should clarify financial arrangements (including any audit fees, lab charges, and computer usage fees) before the visitor leaves China.

A program recently implemented at the request of the Chinese government produces what the Chinese sometimes refer to as "sandwich" degrees. These involve cooperative doctoral programs between U.S. and Chinese institutions in which Chinese students take some courses in the United States, additional courses in China, and complete their dissertations in China. Students in these programs might receive a degree from either or both institutions.

Administration of U.S. Standardized Admissions Tests in China

Officials of the Educational Testing Service and the China International Examinations Coordination Bureau (CIECB) of the State Education Commission of China signed an agreement on May 11, 1981 under which the Test of English as a Foreign Language (TOEFL) and the Graduate Record Examination (GRE) would be offered in the People's Republic of China as of December 1981. The CIECB was appointed by the State Education Commission (then the Ministry of Education) to administer the tests.

Since the initial administration of TOEFL and the GRE in December 1981, much progress has been made in the administration of U.S. standardized admissions tests. In 1982 and 1983, the Graduate Management Admission Test (GMAT) and the Test of Spoken English (TSE) were introduced in China, and the number of centers where tests are administered grew from 3 to 32. Each year, more than 20,000 students take TOEFL, 3,000 to 4,000 students take the GRE, and a small number take the TSE and GMAT. TOEFL is given three times per year. In Shanghai, 2,000 students are tested each time, in Guangzhou, 750 students, and in Beijing, more than 2,000 students.

In the 1988–89 year, the GMAT, GRE and TOEFL/TSE will be administered in Beijing (14 centers), Chengdu, Chongqing, Dalian, Guangzhou, Hangzhou (two centers), Harbin, Hefei, Jinan, Kunming, Nanjing, Shanghai (two centers), Tianjin, Wuhan (two centers), Xiamen, and Xi'an. (See Appendix D for the addresses of the testing sites.) The schedule of the exams is as follows:

TOEFL/TSE
(Test of English as a Foreign Language)
(Test of Spoken English)

Test Date	Registration Closing Date	Score Report Mailing Date
October 22, 1988	September 5, 1988	November 23, 1988
January 14, 1989	November 28, 1988	February 15, 1989
May 13, 1989	March 27, 1989	June 14, 1989

GMAT
(Graduate Management Admission Test)

Test Date	Registration Closing Date	Score Report Mailing Date
October 15, 1988	August 24, 1988	Approximately five
January 28, 1989	December 7, 1988	weeks after the test
March 18, 1989	January 25, 1989	date

GRE
(Graduate Record Examination)

Test Date	Registration Closing Date	Score Report Mailing Date
October 8, 1988	August 22, 1988	December 2, 1988
February 4, 1989	December 12, 1988	March 31, 1989
April 8, 1989	February 20, 1989	June 2, 1989

The exams are administered in China in the same manner as they are throughout the world, with the instructions given in English. The Educational Testing Service adheres to its regular procedures in scoring the tests and reporting test scores.

Students who have received permission to apply to study in the United States or Canada are eligible to take the exams (see page 129). In addition, all privately sponsored students taking the GMAT, GRE, or TOEFL/TSE examinations must pay the registration fee with a U.S.-dollar check drawn on a U.S. bank. Registration fees for officially sponsored students are paid by the Chinese government. Students privately sponsored (by friends or relatives outside China) should be sent a U.S.-dollar check drawn on a U.S. bank by their sponsor. The check should be made payable to CIECB/GMAT, CIECB/GRE, CIECB/TOEFL, or CIECB/TSE, whichever is appropriate, in the following amounts:

- GMAT—$32
- GRE (general *or* special subject)—$39

- GRE (general *and* special subject)—$68
- TOEFL—$29
- TSE—$60

TOEFL/TSE registration fees can be paid with a single check if the applicant registers for the two tests on the combined TOEFL/TSE registration form.

Chinese applicants who wish to take the GMAT, GRE, or TOEFL/TSE test should obtain the appropriate *Bulletin of Information* and registration materials from one of the testing centers listed in Appendix D. Applicants must submit their completed registration forms and payment to the testing center at which they plan to take the test. If a Chinese edition of the *Bulletin* is not available at the testing center, applicants should write to the China International Examinations Coordination Bureau, #30 Yuquan Road, 100039, Beijing, People's Republic of China.

Evaluation of Chinese Academic Credentials

The following information is based on a sampling of credentials received from the PRC by U.S. institutions.

Experience to date shows that most applicants from China can provide fairly complete academic records, with English translations routinely included. Some records may be copies of originals, some appear to be careful reconstructions by a professor or a school official, and some are prepared by officials of the institution with which the applicant is now affiliated. Records are verified by a red stamp.

Grading scales seem to conform to one of three or four patterns familiar to U.S. admissions officers. Credentials received sometimes include explanations of the grading scales. U.S. admissions officers familiar with Chinese transcripts have formulated the following equivalency chart:

90–100	Excellent	A	5
80–89	Very Good	B	4
70–79	Good	C	3
60–69	Pass	D	2
0–59	Fail	F	1

Descriptive titles such as "Q" (qualified) and "U" (unqualified) are sometimes used; records occasionally state that courses were given on a "CR/NCR" (credit/no credit) basis. Individual subjects are sometimes graded on a "Pass/Fail" basis: these usually are in continuing or laboratory courses that do not require a final examination. It is not unusual to find more than one of the foregoing scales in use on the same transcript.

At the college level, educators in China estimate that 20 percent of all grades fall in the range of 90 to 100; only five percent may fail a course. Failure is rare—the system is so selective, the rewards so great. On a visit to China, a U.S. university administrator learned from Chinese counterparts that a student who fails an exam three times would be dismissed, but sensed that this had never happened.

High school (senior middle-school) records for study before 1966 give the subjects, grades, and number of hours of study. Credentials that include a period of study during the Cultural Revolution (1966–76) normally are accompanied by explanatory notes. Some applicants state that all their academic records were lost during this period; such individuals should be asked to reconstruct their educational history as accurately and completely as possible. Work done at the graduate level during this period will be the hardest to track, because graduate instruction often took place at research institutes where there was no "official" coursework and no grades were recorded. Such persons should be asked to submit accounts of their research, any publications, and evaluations from their instructors. It should be determined if such applicants now are enrolled in Chinese graduate programs or employed on university faculties. If they are not, their professional status should be clarified and evaluated in reference to their academic goals.

The Chinese now maintain complete middle-school and college records and prepare transcripts recording work performed. Middle-school graduation certificates often include grades of the National College Entrance Examination, showing scores on the required exams and the foreign language test. The university to which the student was accepted in China also may be stated. Scores of the national examinations should be requested from all applicants. These scores may not be available in an official report form, but they are known to the applicant and should be self-reported. If the exams were not taken, the applicant's educational history should be carefully evaluated to determine whether college level placement should be considered.

While U.S. educational terminology often is used in the English translations of transcripts from the PRC, the use of familiar terms can be unintentionally misleading. For example, one record quoting by subject and letter grades on the "Graduate Record Exam" refers to China's own graduate entrance exam, not the U.S. Graduate Record Examination. Admissions officers may find that it is the current employer of the applicant who provides academic documents requested by the U.S. institution.

Placement Recommendations for Academic Credentials from the People's Republic of China*

Primary school: five to six years of education
Junior middle-school: three years of education (There are some experimental four-year programs.)
The goal is nine years of primary and junior middle education representing compulsory schooling.

Credential	Minimum Entrance Requirements	Length of Study	Placement Recommendations
Secondary Education			
Agricultural Junior Secondary School Diploma	primary school	3–4 years	primarily a vocational credential; placement in adult secondary school may be appropriate
Senior Middle-School Diploma			
1. pre-1966	6 + 3 years primary and junior middle-school	3 years	may be considered for freshman admission, but may need refresher courses
2. 1967–77	5 + 3 years primary and junior middle-school	2 years	admission and placement should be based on other academic credentials; not eligible for freshman admission with only this credential
3. 1978–present	5 + 3 years primary and secondary (changing to 6 + 3 years)	3 years (2 years in many schools until mid-1980s)	may be considered for freshman admission (See text for discussions of National College Entrance Examination scores.)

Credential	Minimum Entrance Requirements	Length of Study	Placement Recommendations
Technical School Diploma	completion of junior middle-school or senior middle-school diploma	3 years or 2 years	may be considered for freshman admission where specialized training is considered appropriate preparation
Vocational School Diploma	completion of junior middle-school	2–3 years	primarily a vocational credential; placement in adult secondary school may be appropriate
Specialized Secondary School Diploma	completion of junior middle-school	3 years	may be considered for freshman admission
Primary School Teacher Certificate	completion of junior middle-school or senior middle-school diploma	3–4 years or 2 years	may be considered for freshman admission where specialized training is appropriate preparation

University Education

Students who have completed some coursework for any of the programs listed below may be considered for undergraduate (or graduate) admission with up to a maximum of 30 semester hours of transfer credit for each year, determined through a course-by-course analysis. When the length of a program is cited, it refers to the standard length of the program when pursued full time. The actual period of attendance may vary.

Credential	Minimum Entrance Requirements	Length of Study	Placement Recommendations
College, university, or institute diploma awarded before 1966 and 1978–82 or bachelor's degree since 1982	pre-1966—national entrance examination; since 1978, National College Entrance Examination	4 years (some 5-year programs)	may be considered for graduate admission

Credential	Minimum Entrance Requirements	Length of Study	Placement Recommendations
College, university, or institute diploma awarded before 1966–77	recommendation of the work unit	3 years	admission and placement should be based on academic credentials, professional experience, and examination
Physician or Dentist diploma; since 1982, Bachelor's Degree in Medicine or Dentistry	National College Entrance Exam	5 years	may be considered to have a degree comparable to the first professional degree in the field; may be considered for graduate admission
Graduate Study Diploma Pre–1966 or 1978–81	undergraduate diploma and/or graduate entrance exam	2–3 years	may be considered for graduate admission with graduate transfer credit determined after evaluation of at least one semester of graduate work in the United States
Master's Degree	bachelor's degree and/or graduate entrance exam	2–3 years	may be considered comparable to a U.S. master's degree
Doctor's Degree	master's degree and entrance exam	3 years	may be considered comparable to a U.S. earned doctorate
Credentials for Foreign Students			
Certificate of Advanced Study for General Advanced Student	2 years undergraduate education in China or foreign university	1–2 years in same field or elementary Chinese	may be considered for undergraduate transfer credit determined through course-by-course analysis

Credential	Minimum Entrance Requirements	Length of Study	Placement Recommendations
Certificate of Advanced Study for Senior Advanced Student	master's degree or candidate for foreign doctorate	1 year advanced independent study	may be considered for graduate transfer credit

Nontraditional Education

Credential	Minimum Entrance Requirements	Length of Study	Placement Recommendations
Radio and Television University Graduation Diploma (certificate = completion of subject)	entrance exam (also independent enrollment with no entrance exam)	2–3 years	admission and placement should be based on academic credentials, professional experience, and examination

Adult Education: certificate, diploma, records

1. education for peasants—literacy training, technical secondary education			admission and placement should be based on other credentials
2. education for workers and staff members—professional training offered at primary, secondary, and higher education levels Higher education = worker and spare-time universities (3 years for work release, 4 years spare time)			
3. cadre education, including administrative colleges			
4. correspondence and evening universities			

*Prepared by Karlene N. Dickey (Stanford University) and approved by the national team of the Admissions Section of the National Association for Foreign Student Affairs.

117

Based on extensive experience evaluating Chinese academic credentials, the national team of the Admissions Section of NAFSA outlined the following placement recommendations for Chinese students in October 1986.

Because television and spare-time universities may present some problems to admissions officers, the following advice is offered by G. James Haas of Indiana University for assessing credentials received from those type universities.

- Even though some of the students are not middle-school graduates, if they passed an examination to enroll in a television university, they should be compared to students in the United States who did not complete high school but later passed a General Educational Development (GED) exam.
- If an employer is paying the tuition/fees and also giving released work time to an employee, U.S. institutions can be assured that the enrollment is being taken very seriously.

A U.S. evaluator should still use common sense in reviewing television-conducted study. It is highly likely that English courses would be of an English-as-a-second-language nature, and thus may not warrant degree credit at a U.S. institution. It is recommended that all courses from television universities be assessed on a course-by-course basis. A certificate/diploma from a television university should not be equated to a B.A./B.S. degree.

In assessing individual courses, care should be given in assigning semester credit values. Television-university academic records frequently do not assign a credit-hour value to the individual courses passed; the U.S. evaluator will need to make his or her own determination of credit value. Additional clock and calendar time will likely be needed by television university students to make up for the absence of libraries, laboratories, and personal contact with instructors. An evaluator should view television courses in China as being worth the same as similar courses conducted in the United States. The student should be asked to write an eight- to ten-line description in English of the materials covered in each course. Equipped with this information, the U.S. evaluator can address the question of advanced standing/transfer credit. Some students of spare-time universities who apply to U.S. institutions of higher education may have expertise in a certain field gained through study elsewhere and are attending a spare-time university primarily for English-language training.

Two other items may be of possible assistance to admissions personnel evaluating credentials from China.

1. It has been noted by some U.S. admissions officers that a few forged documents, particularly letters of reference, are beginning to be received from Chinese applicants. Personnel in the Education Division of the Chinese Embassy in Washington, DC report that any student found to have submitted forged documents to a U.S. institution, would be in serious trouble back home.

2. Some U.S. admissions personnel have received letters from Chinese applicants stating that while they have been enrolled in one university's graduate program, their degree was conferred by another university. Education Division personnel say this is possible, since some institutions do not have authorization to issue degrees. They warn, however, that caution should be exerted in these cases, as it is not a frequent occurrence, and recommend that a photocopy of the degree and an explanation of the situation be requested from the applicant.

English-Language Ability

English Levels of Chinese Students and Scholars in the United States. Administrators at U.S. institutions of higher education report that Chinese students and scholars arriving on U.S. campuses today communicate much more effectively in English than those who arrived in the late 1970s and early 1980s. This phenomenon is due no doubt to the improvement in English teaching in China that is described below. Nevertheless, foreign student advisers surveyed in 1981 and 1984 reported that many Chinese students arriving in the United States require additional English-language training through coursework before they can successfully handle other academic pursuits. Aural comprehension is the most common language deficiency of both Chinese students and scholars, but limited speaking ability is reported almost as often. Students have more problems with writing ability and grammar than do visiting scholars; the opposite is true with respect to vocabulary. Reading comprehension seems to cause the least difficulties for both students and scholars.

Teaching of English in China. The teaching of English in China begins in primary schools in grade six and continues through middle school in grades 7 through 12. The National College Entrance Examination includes a section testing English-language proficiency; depending upon their performance on the college entrance examination, students receive from two to four more years of English-language instruction at the university level. If necessary, two years of general English-language instruction, which emphasizes the study of literary classics and readings in current events with minimal concentration on oral/aural skills, is provided. All university students receive two years of technical English in their major field.

Both Chinese and foreign instructors teach general English courses. Technical English often is taught by Chinese professors whose speciality is not English. Chinese teachers of English are being trained in special language institutes, university departments of foreign languages, and normal colleges. In addition, there are special "spare time" English classes for those not enrolled in regular school. English teaching programs are broadcast on Chinese radio and television, and the Voice of America, which is widely listened to in China, also broadcasts special English-learning programs.

Nine language-training and predeparture orientation centers have been established throughout China since 1979 (see Appendix C). Eight of these centers are under the jurisdiction of the Bureau of Foreign Affairs of the State Education Commission. They generally prepare government-sponsored students and scholars for study or research abroad by providing foreign-language training, an introduction to foreign cultures, instruction on being a good representative of China, and information about passports, visas, scholarships, and overseas institutions. The ninth center is run cooperatively by the Institute of International Education and Guangdong Province. It assists Chinese students and scholars in learning about the U.S. education system and academic life in the United States.

The eight SEDC training centers provide six months to one year of English-language instruction to approximately 1,100 students and scholars bound for the United States each year. The majority of the students are recent college graduates with outstanding academic records who usually have had two years of English as undergraduate students; they are either planning to go overseas to continue their studies or conduct research, or are being trained to become English teachers. At the centers, they are given between 20 and 30 hours per week of classroom English instruction. Students and scholars attend separate language classes.

The centers have no uniform curriculum, so quality varies from one to another. Some centers make active use of foreign teachers whose native language is English (or other target language).

Some of the centers were developed with assistance from institutions in the United States, Australia, and Canada, or the United Nations Development Program. The curricula and materials emphasize communication skills. Five areas are covered: reading, listening, speaking, writing, and the culture of the target country. Two of the training centers visited by NAFSA delegations in China are described below.

Shanghai International Studies University (formerly Shanghai Foreign Languages Institute). This center trains students and scholars in English, French, German, and Russian. There are two English programs, one for six months and one for 12 months. Instruction is provided at only one level, although students are grouped according to their score on an English examination taken prior to entry. The top 20 are in one class, the second 20 in another class, and so on. There are 20 to 30 hours per week of instruction in speaking/listening, reading, writing, and technical English. U.S. culture is introduced, and students watch movies, television, and videos outside class. At the end of the program, students take TOEFL. In addition to these programs conducted for the State Education Commission, this center has developed programs for the British Council (a nine-month course for graduate students going to the United Kingdom) and for the United Nations Development Program (a six-month course for non-academic short-term visitors).

Zhongshan University. This university has two language training centers: Chinese for foreign students and English for Chinese going abroad. The English-training center, called the Guangzhou English Language Center, was established with assistance from the University of California at Los Angeles. The program offers ten weeks of instruction at three levels of proficiency, focusing on English for specific purposes (science and technology), English as a second language, and English for academic purposes. Reading, writing, speaking/listening, technical English, and U.S. culture are studied by students, who attend classes six hours per day. Instruction is given in lectures, small-group discussions, and language labs. To enroll in the center, students must have completed the general English program at the university and have a TOEFL score of at least 450. The average TOEFL score upon completion of the program is 540. When the center first opened, U.S. commercial and public resource materials were used; these now have been replaced by materials developed especially for the center by Chinese and American faculty. In the 1985–86 academic year, there were seven foreign teachers on the staff at the center.

Other English-language training centers were established by the Bell Educational Trust, a nonprofit British educational foundation based in Cambridge, England, at the Beijing Forestry University and Huazhong University in Wuhan in 1983. The centers were designed to train Chinese graduate students of agriculture and related disciplines in the general, social, and academic English needed for them to pursue postgraduate studies in English-medium institutions of higher education. Most of the graduates of the centers continue their studies in the

United States, but other destinations include Great Britain, Canada, Australia, the Philippines, and (occasionally) Italy and Switzerland. Students are admitted on the basis of a screening test administered under the auspices of the ministries of agriculture and forestry; those in the Beijing center are drawn from all over northern China; students in the Wuhan center come from southern China. There are a maximum of 120 students at each center at any one time. They follow an eight-month intensive course in blocks of 10 or 11 weeks each. Courses include English for science and technology, general language skills, social English, study skills, academic writing, video/seminar courses in which students learn how to participate in seminars, project work, and conversational topics. They also offer classes for students preparing to take the TOEFL test during the month prior to each examination.

Students at the Bell Educational Trust centers are assessed in two ways: by continual assessment (standardized as far as possible by the use of progress tests, assessment scales, and cross-marking of oral and written work) and by formal tests, which have been developed in China by Bell employees. When a student graduates from a center, he or she is given an overall assessment grade (ETA) on an eight-point scale from zero to eight, eight being a highly educated native-speaker level. Most of the graduates of the centers fall between 5.0 and 6.0. If a student has a score of 5.5, he or she will be able to cope with graduate studies with little difficulty; grades of 5.0 to 5.4 probably mean that a student will need tutorial assistance. Students are issued a Language Ability Certificate that details what they can do in the four skill areas of English and study skills; indications also are provided about what a student cannot do.

The U.S. government sponsors a limited number of English and American studies teachers in China under the Fulbright Program. China also is actively recruiting U.S. teachers to teach in China (see Chapter 16).

English Language Testing in China. TOEFL and the TSE are administered in China now (see Administration of U.S. Standardized Admissions Tests in China, p. 110). Students may still have difficulty in obtaining a testing place, but the number of centers where TOEFL/TSE are administered is constantly expanding. Students may also have difficulty obtaining U.S. dollars to pay the registration fee if it is not provided by their sponsor; however, the number of individuals who have taken TOEFL indicates that it is possible to obtain the fee. For additional information about the administration of TOEFL and the TSE in China, contact the Test of English as a Foreign Language, Educational Testing Service, Princeton, NJ 08541-6155, phone: 609/921-9000.

In addition, the Michigan English Language Assessment Battery (MELAB) is administered in China on an individual or group basis. (The Michigan Test of English Language Proficiency is a 100-item grammar, vocabulary, and reading test that was one part of the Michigan Test Battery previously administered in China. Since 1985, the name of the total battery has been changed to the Michigan English Language Assessment Battery.) The official MELAB is offered only through the English Language Institute of the University of Michigan. All MELAB tests now are administered in China under the supervision of the China International Examinations Coordination Bureau (CIECB). The test battery includes a written composition, a tape-recorded listening test, and a multiple-choice test of grammar, cloze, vocabulary, and reading. An additional oral interview is optional.

The MELAB tests are administered by official examiners located in the following 11 cities: Beijing (Ministry of Machine Building Industry, Institute of Managerial Cadres—group and individual—and Institute of Aeronautics and Astronautics—group only); Chengdu (Chengdu University of Science and Technology); Guangzhou (South China Normal University); Harbin (Harbin Institute of Technology); Kunming (Yunnan University); Shanghai (Shanghai Jiaotong University); Shenyang (Liaoning University); Tianjin (Nankai University); Wuhan (Wuhan University); Xiamen (Xiamen University); and Xi'an (Xi'an Medical University). All test papers are graded at the Testing and Certification Division of the English Language Institute in Ann Arbor, Michigan. Score reports are issued only by the Testing and Certification Division. One copy of the score report is sent to the candidate. Two additional score reports can be authorized at the time of the test to be sent to universities or colleges. Additional score reports, or any score reports ordered later, cost U.S. $3 each. Normal turnaround time for group tests in China from applicant registration to issuance of score reports is approximately six weeks. Test papers generally arrive at the English Language Institute ten days after test administration. Admissions officers who urgently require test scores may telephone the testing division at 313/764-2416 to make arrangements to rush the scoring of tests. To be eligible to take the test, the candidate must not have taken the Michigan Test Battery within the last six weeks or taken the test more than three times within the last 12 months.

Group tests are scheduled three times per year: in mid-April, mid-June, and mid-December. Candidates should go to one of the 12 examination centers in China to register. The fee for the group test is U.S. $25 (or $30 if an oral interview is to be included). The fee should be in the form of a check written on the Bank of China, made payable to the CIECB. When they register, candidates fill out a registration form and an identification form and submit two recent photos. When they take the test, candidates must bring an identification that includes a photo (passport or employee, student, or national identity card) to confirm their identity.

Under special circumstances, individual tests can be scheduled at the convenience of the candidate and local examiner. Applications for an individual test can be requested from the English Language Institute. Once received, the candidate completes the individual application form and sends it, with the required fee of U.S. $30 (U.S. $35 if an oral interview is to be included), to the English Language Institute at the University of Michigan. The English Language Institute will send the candidate authorization to be tested, which includes information about whom to contact for the test. The authorization is valid for six months. The candidate needs to complete the identification form on the reverse of the authorization and take it to the test, along with two recent photos and a passport or national identity card as supporting photo evidence of his or her identity. Candidates whose tests have been requested by a sponsoring organization, such as the World Health Organization or the United Nations Development Program, do not need to pay fees or register for the test. The sponsor will pay all fees and register the candidate for the test. For more information about the administration of the MELAB in China, contact the English Language Institute, Testing and Certification Division, University of Michigan, Ann Arbor, MI 48109-1057, phone: 313/764-2416 or 763-3452.

Other methods used to assess the English-language skills of Chinese applicants include evaluations by a native speaker of English who knows the applicant, interviews in China by visiting U.S. faculty members, requests for detailed summaries of English study, letters of evaluation from Chinese English instructors, and evaluations of statements written by candidates as part of the application process. Several programs organized in specific disciplines also help outstanding Chinese students and scholars come to the United States. Three of these programs are the China-U.S. Biochemistry Examination and Application (CUSBEA) Program, China-U.S. Physics Examination and Application (CUSPEA) Program, and Mathematics Program. They are described in the NAFSA publication *China Update #6: China-U.S. Examination and Application Programs*.

Several Chinese English-language tests have been developed to assess the English-language ability of Chinese students and scholars. Among them are the English Proficiency Test (EPT) and the Visiting Scholars Test (VST). The latter test has been eliminated. The EPT, revised in 1987, is given twice each year, in May / June and December. It will be used only to screen students going abroad under Chinese or other government funding. If students receive a qualifying grade on the EPT, they will then take the Test of English as a Foreign Language (TOEFL). Therefore, U.S. institutions should not receive EPT scores from students in China. If they do, they should not accept them. Rather, they should require that the student take TOEFL. The EPT, which follows the TOEFL format, contains five sections: listening comprehension, grammar, reading comprehension, essay writing, and cloze. Each section is scored individually; the maximum score possible on the EPT is 160. The total time of the test is less than two hours. It is not possible to equate EPT and TOEFL scores.

If students have not been able to take TOEFL in China, they should be tested for English after arrival at the U.S. institution. Applicants should be told that this testing will take place and forewarned that additional English instruction may be required, with indications of the time and fees this coursework will entail. The U.S. Embassy and consulates in China are not prepared to administer English proficiency tests, but consular personnel may refuse to issue a visa if the applicant does not demonstrate a reasonable command of English and his or her Certificate of Eligibility does not indicate that remedial instruction in English will be provided as necessary.

Financial Support

Chinese students and scholars come to the United States as either officially sponsored or privately sponsored individuals. There are several sources that provide funding for government or officially sponsored Chinese students and scholars. These include the State Education Commission and other ministries at the national level, the World Bank, provincial and municipal governments, and individual work units. Privately sponsored students are supported either by friends or relatives, usually in the United States or a third country, or by U.S. academic institutions.

In recent years, U.S. academic institutions have expressed concern about two areas of support provided to officially sponsored students and scholars: the adequacy of monthly maintenance allowances and the renewability of Chinese awards from year to year.

The standard stipend provided to officially sponsored students and scholars is $5,000 per year, $380 to $440 per month plus a modest book allowance of up to $300 per year. This amount is intended to pay for room, board, and insurance costs. It does not include tuition or other institutional fees such as laboratory, activities, or academic fees.

The issue of the adequacy of monthly stipends is extremely complex, with many cultural and social implications. Representatives of the State Education Commission have said that they would review the possibility of increasing the general level of stipends and of providing limited additional funding to allow scholars to attend professional meetings. However, there is not much enthusiasm for a change in policy, for the following reasons:

1. The Chinese government is providing more than just monthly stipends to their students and scholars in the United States. It pays international travel costs and salaries to families at home, as well as living stipends, spending approximately $7,500 per year per student or scholar.

2. Increasing the maintenance allowance would decrease the number of students and scholars the Chinese government could fund for study or research abroad.

3. Government representatives believe that if the stipends are increased, the students and scholars will not spend the extra funds on improving their living conditions in the United States, but will save more money to purchase consumer goods to take back to China upon completion of their programs.

The Chinese government awards scholarships for a one-year period and encourages students and scholars whom they sponsor to secure teaching or research assistantships or other forms of scholarships from U.S. sources for the funds they will need after the first year. Beginning in 1985, all letters outlining the financial support from an official source in China were to be sent by the State Education Commission, which has designed standardized letters for this purpose. However, it is taking some time for this process to be implemented, and a number of U.S. institutions have reported that they still are receiving such letters directly from Chinese universities. Only key universities are authorized to send letters of financial support if they have been given a quota from the State Education Commission to send students or scholars to the United States. If letters received state that only one year of funding will be provided, that is exactly the intent. However, a second year of funding is possible, and perhaps even a third year, depending on a number of circumstances, including the field of study or research. For example, students or scholars in social sciences, humanities, and English may be able to receive money for a longer period of time, since the State Education Commission realizes that it is difficult to obtain funding in the United States in those fields.

If U.S. institutions have questions about funding for a prospective Chinese student or scholar, the individual's home institution should be contacted to ask if support can be provided for a second or third year. The Chinese institution will then contact the State Education Commission to see if it will authorize a longer period of support. Individual Chinese universities can only authorize up to one year of funding. Staff of the Education Division of the Embassy of the People's Republic of China (2300 Connecticut Avenue, N.W., Washington, DC 20008) will also provide assistance to U.S. institutions having problems with the level of stipends of Chinese students and scholars.

Since the Chinese government has decentralized the awarding of scholarships and many ministries less familiar with all expenses that must be covered by scholarships are now involved in the process, U.S. institutions might wish to be very specific about the amounts of money needed by Chinese students and scholars when they communicate with sponsors in China. For example, it would be helpful if specific amounts were listed that are needed for tuition, fees, and books; room and board; and monthly living expenses. In this way, the Chinese agency awarding the scholarship would have all the information necessary to determine the appropriate award level and length.

Scholarships are awarded to Chinese students and scholars on a specific schedule. Scholarship applicants are chosen by examinations given in the summer. They are notified if they will receive funding in the fall. The State Education Commission realizes that they will not begin to attend a U.S. institution until the following year. This schedule is followed by all sources of funding in China with one possible exception—students who receive funding from money loaned to China by the World Bank. It is understood by Chinese Embassy personnel that funding from the World Bank must be used in the same year in which it is awarded.

Chinese authorities encourage their students to seek financial assistance from sources outside China because of the high cost of U.S. higher education, the present economic situation in the PRC, and the difficulties in obtaining foreign currency. The students have been extremely successful in doing so: according to a survey conducted by the U.S. Embassy in Beijing in 1986, U.S. academic institutions award more than $100 million to Chinese students and scholars per year.

The Chinese government provides some incentives to privately sponsored students. If these students receive a higher degree than a B.A./B.S. abroad, the Chinese government will assist them with their international travel expenses home. Once the students have returned to China, the Chinese government also will provide financial assistance if they have difficulties locating employment. Privately sponsored students have the same privileges as government-sponsored students regarding such assistance. Certainly more students from

China are now privately sponsored by friends or relatives than was the case at the beginning of U.S.-China educational exchanges. However, the level and continuation of this support once the student is in the United States have not been without problems.

U.S. admissions officers must clearly be alert to possible problems with financial assistance for Chinese students and scholars. If a Chinese student or scholar is being officially sponsored, it is useful to obtain precise information about the amount of money that will be provided by the sponsor and for what length of time. If a recruitment agency is given as the source of financial support, admissions officers should check with the Foreign Student Recruitment Information Clearinghouse of NAFSA for additional information about the agency. If a Chinese student is being privately sponsored, financial support letters should include all the information required by the U.S. Embassy and consulates in China (see Chapter 14).

Other

Chinese Government Regulations Affecting Study Abroad. The following general Chinese government regulations affecting study abroad were determined at a conference of Chinese educators and government officials in May 1986 and are affirmed in the regulations issued by the Chinese government in June 1987:

1. If students pass the Chinese National College Entrance Examination and are admitted to a Chinese university, they *must* attend that institution in China. If they do not take the examination or do not do well enough on the exam to be admitted to a Chinese institution, but are accepted by a U.S. institution and have financial support, they will be issued a passport and be allowed to study abroad.

2. Students at the undergraduate or graduate levels in China must complete their full program of study in China before requesting permission to apply for study abroad. When they have completed their studies, graduated, and worked for a specified period of time in China, they can apply, with permission from their work unit—the university, research institute, or job to which they have been assigned—to study abroad.

3. After students graduate from a program of study in China, either graduate or undergraduate, the Chinese government wishes them to do practical work in China related to their studies so their time abroad will be more worthwhile and their work in China upon return will be more productive. This policy applies to all students wishing to go abroad, regardless of sponsorship. The length of time students must

work in China varies depending on their course of study. It may be six months to five years or no time at all: there is no overall government regulation about the specific time-period required to work in China before going overseas to study. Work units have now been given more power in determining who will be permitted to go abroad to study and at what time. Exceptions to the rule of working in China before going abroad to study are made in critical need areas. Maturity also is a determining factor in the length of time required for work in China: while some students can apply for study abroad at an early age, others need to wait until they are older and more mature.

4. The age of applicants sponsored by the Chinese government for undergraduate or graduate studies abroad must not be over 35, and for scholars not over 45.

5. All students previously sponsored by the Chinese government were selected by the State Education Commission. Applicants were given a special exam to qualify them for study abroad. This situation has changed. Now, the State Education Commission each year informs various ministries, institutions, and other agencies that they have a certain number of students they can send abroad at the government's expense. The sponsoring unit chooses the students it wants to send abroad and the fields they want them to study. The unit can give exams that it designs to a number of students in order to select the ones who finally will be sent abroad.

6. Several years ago, students could select their field of study themselves. Now the students chosen to study abroad must discuss with their sponsor what they will study and must study those subjects when they go abroad. This practice reflects a change of policy by the Chinese government. Whereas formerly they selected good students to send abroad and then found them suitable jobs upon return to China, they now look at the kinds of jobs they will have to offer students when they return and then select them accordingly.

7. Students who come to the United States have a contract with their unit that requires them to return to China upon completion of their academic work and guarantees them a job in the work unit. These contracts are an attempt to define clearly the duties and responsibilities of both the sending organization and the student, including the length and subject of overseas study and (on occasion) the student's commitment to work for a specified period of time in the sender's work unit following his or her studies. For example, officially sponsored students who attain their doctoral degrees overseas are now required to return to China to work for a period to repay the Chinese investment in their education before being allowed to go to a third country for further education. Contracts written by the State Education Commis-

sion do not include financial damages for breach of contract, although other sending parties, including regional, provincial, and municipal government entities, often design their own contracts to include punitive financial measures. The State Education Commission has openly opposed this trend.

8. The Chinese government is giving preference to Ph.D. candidates who wish to study abroad rather than to master's degree candidates, as it is believed that appropriate master's degrees can now be obtained in China.

Payment of Application Fees. Payment of application fees is sometimes a problem for applicants from the PRC because of limited access to foreign exchange. Nevertheless, the majority of U.S. institutions have reported that they are requiring applicants from China to pay normal application fees. These fees are received from Chinese students after arrival in the United States, from other sources outside China (particularly in the case of privately sponsored students), from departments at the U.S. institution to which the student has been admitted, through loans from international student offices which must be repaid after arrival, and, in a few cases, in the form of foreign exchange remitted from China.

Definitive information about how foreign exchange is obtained in China is difficult to obtain. However, representatives of the Bank of China in New York have said that the regulations regarding conversion of *renminbi* into foreign currency are determined by the Bureau (or Commission) of Foreign Currency Control. There are three kinds of accounts: A, B, and C. C accounts are the most flexible; currencies can be converted and sent out of the country with no stipulations. B accounts are more restrictive; A accounts require specific permission to send foreign currency out of the country. A further difference in foreign currency accounts is that some require U.S.-dollar cash deposits and others, checks or non-cash remittances. This difference does not apparently alter the condition of whether foreign currency can be sent out of China with or without a letter of permission. Additional information provided by staff of the Education Division of the Chinese Embassy in Washington, DC indicates that foreign currency must be declared when a person enters China. This can be deposited in a foreign-currency account. Money can then be withdrawn from the account in a foreign currency. It thus appears that a person must have taken some foreign currency into China at some time before being able to obtain it. An exception to this is made for privately sponsored Chinese students, who can receive permission to convert *renminbi* into U.S. dollars (a maximum of approximately $100) once they have obtained a U.S. visa—long after the time they would need U.S. dollars to pay an application fee.

Correspondence with Applicants. As Chinese applicants may be unfamiliar with the procedures for leaving China, admissions letters to Chinese students and scholars should explain the need to take the I-20 or IAP-66 and all relevant letters and documents to the U.S. Embassy or consulate when the student or scholar applies for a U.S. visa. Long delays have been experienced in processing applications from China, due partly to government bureaucracy (U.S. and Chinese) and partially to the mail. Airmail letters between the United States and China take between four days and two weeks. Letters should be addressed to the "People's Republic of China"; the country name must not be abbreviated. An address written in Chinese characters speeds the process by several days, especially in areas outside the larger cities. Addresses using Chinese characters must also have the addressee's name and city name followed by "People's Republic of China" written in English so it can be handled accurately by the U.S. post office. Writing the address in pinyin rather than Wade-Giles will reduce the chance of delivery error. (A *Pinyin* Romanization pronunciation guide to common Chinese surnames and *Pinyin* names of provinces and major cities are given in Appendix E; a map of China is reproduced in Appendix F.)

Terminology Guidelines for China. The following guidelines, issued by the U.S. Department of State in August 1981, provide the official U.S. government policy on terminology used for the People's Republic of China and Taiwan.

The United States government acknowledges the Chinese position that there is only one China, of which Taiwan is a part. Taiwan is not considered a separate country, and should not be referred to as such. The term "Republic of China" is never used by the U.S. government in reference to Taiwan.

Lists of economic statistics, indices, and similar materials prepared by the U.S. government list "China" (not People's Republic of China) in its proper alphabetical position. This is followed by "Mainland" and then "Taiwan," each indented and printed in a distinctive typeface. Statistics or other material are then given for each listing. However, no totals are given for "China" as an entity.

For non-statistical information, such as visitor lists by country, a listing is made for "China." This is followed by an asterisk and a footnote reading, "See also Taiwan at the end of this listing." "Taiwan" is placed at the end of the country lists, not in alphabetical position

131

under "T." Information on China Mainland is placed directly under "China."

Wherever possible, the term "China" is used in place of "People's Republic of China."

14

Governmental and Institutional Regulations

Passport and Visa Application and Issuance Process

Individuals from the People's Republic of China applying for admission to U.S. institutions or for a position as a visiting scholar follow the same procedures as do other foreign nationals. The prospective student or scholar submits to the U.S. institution his or her credentials and proposed academic programs, and application forms if appropriate. The student or scholar also provides evidence of sufficient financial support to begin pursuit of his or her academic program. If relatives in the United States are sponsoring a Chinese student or scholar, they should provide a notarized, completed Affidavit of Support (Form I-134) or other financial support forms used by the U.S. institution. The U.S. Embassy or consulate in China requires the Form I-134 as part of the visa application. If the U.S. institution decides to admit or receive the applicant, it sends the appropriate Certificate of Eligibility to the student or scholar with the letter of acceptance or invitation.

The decision about which type of Certificate of Eligibility (Form I-20 or Form IAP-66) is appropriate is made by the campus officer responsible for sending these certificates, and is based on the sponsorship of the applicant. (A Form I-20 enables an applicant to receive an F-1 student visa; a Form IAP-66 enables an applicant to receive a J-1 exchange visitor visa.) However, a number of U.S. institutions have been receiving requests from Chinese students for a different type of Certificate of Eligibility than the one issued to them. Regulations released in China in June 1987 state that only undergraduate students and master's degree candidates who are privately sponsored by family or friends may come to the United States on F-1 visas. All scholars and other prospective students, including those who already have obtained a master's degree or have achieved the level of lecturer or above and those sponsored by U.S. institutions, must come to the United States on J-1 visas.

In addition, two types of privately sponsored Chinese students will be required to have Forms IAP-66: those students whose work units only grant leaves of absence for study overseas to those traveling on J-1 visas, and those who have agreed to be "planned students." A "planned student" is one who finds his or her own sources of funding for study abroad but for whom a Chinese sponsor (ministry, institution, etc.) agrees to keep a job open, continues to pay a salary, and provides for resettlement when the student returns from overseas. A student may become a planned student in the following manner. Each year, the State Education Commission assigns a quota to each ministry or other work unit for sending students abroad. The Ministry of Foreign Economic Relations and Trade, for example, might fill the 100 slots it has been assigned. A 101st student seeking support from the ministry can request to become a planned student; he or she will be responsible for finding funding for study abroad, but the ministry will take care of expenses in China.

As defined by the U.S. Department of State, an exchange visitor is anyone participating in a program that has been designated by the U.S. Information Agency as an official exchange-visitor program. Institutions that are uncertain whether they have a designated exchange-visitor program and sponsor's code number should clarify their status with the Office of Exchange Visitor Facilitative Staff, U.S. Information Agency, 301 4th Street, S.W., Room 714, Washington, DC 20415, phone: 202/485-7964.

Chinese applicants have at times requested a specific type of Certificate of Eligibility, or both a Form I-20 and Form IAP-66. There can be a number of reasons for this, including confusion about what the various types of visas indicate and lack of communication about new Chinese government regulations. It may also be a consequence of the regulations and procedures for obtaining a passport from the Chinese government and a visa from the U.S. Embassy or consulate.

When the Chinese student or scholar receives notification of admission to a U.S. institution and a valid Certificate of Eligibility (either an I-20 or IAP-66), he or she applies for a passport from the Chinese government. Applications for passports for students and scholars who have an IAP-66 are made on behalf of the student or scholar by the applicant's work unit and/or sponsor. Such applications are submitted to the Foreign Affairs Ministry or a Provincial Foreign Affairs Office, and take approximately two weeks to one month to process. If a student or scholar being sponsored by a U.S. institution incurs problems obtaining a passport, information should be requested about the applicant's work unit and an appropriate person to contact (e.g., the president or vice president of the university the applicant is presently attending). A letter should be sent to that person verifying that the applicant will be supported financially by the U.S. institution. Students who have an I-20 apply to the local Public Security Bureau for a passport. They must have a letter of permission from their work unit to do so. It takes approximately one to two months to obtain a passport from the Public Security Bureau.

Four types of passports are issued in China:

- *Light brown.* These are for privately sponsored students, scholars, and tourists, and are issued by the Public Security Bureau in the region, province, or municipality.
- *Dark brown.* These are for government-sponsored students, scholars, and business travelers, and are issued by the Ministry of Foreign Affairs.
- *Green.* These are for university officials and others making special visits abroad, such as members of delegations; they are issued by the Ministry of Foreign Affairs.
- *Red.* These are for diplomats and are issued by the Ministry of Foreign Affairs.

Once a passport has been received, the student or scholar takes it, two completed visa application forms, a completed student data sheet (the last two items are available from the U.S. Embassy and consulates), two recent photographs one and one-half inches square, a valid Form I-20 or Form IAP-66, evidence of educational background (including diplomas and transcripts), and an official statement indicating the availability of sufficient financial support to begin the desired academic program (from Chinese, U.S., or other sources) to the U.S. Embassy or nearest consulate to apply for a visa. As of June 1988, U.S. missions in China included the U.S. Embassy in Beijing and U.S. consulates in Chengdu, Guangzhou, Shanghai, and Shenyang. (See Appendix G for addresses and phone numbers.)

To establish sufficiency of financial support, students or scholars applying for a J-1 visa who are sponsored by the Chinese government, U.S. government, U.S. institution, or private organization must present an official letter or document showing the amount of financial support that has been awarded. If that amount is insufficient to cover all anticipated expenses, the applicant also must provide evidence that additional funds are available from other sources. Students applying for an F-1 visa who are sponsored by friends or relatives in the United States or a third country must present from the sponsor a notarized, completed Form I-134 Affidavit of Support, and employment history (including name of employer and a copy of a recent income tax form) or bank statements showing amount, duration, and type of accounts.

Foreign student advisers should be certain that the sponsor intends to make the funds available to the student or scholar. Unfortunately, some people in China mistakenly believe that a foreign student can easily earn his or her keep in the United States. Prospective sponsors should be reminded that U.S. law limits employment opportunities of foreign students. U.S. immigration regulations require that F-1 visa holders carry a full academic program. Under the terms of their visas, foreign students are not permitted to accept off-campus employment during the first year of study in the United States. Thereafter, a student may qualify for off-campus employment only if demonstrated unforeseen changes in financial circumstances arising after arrival in the United States necessitate working for purposes of self-support and the student shows that he or she can manage a part-time job without adversely affecting his or her studies, which must be continued on a full-time basis. Both the U.S. institution and the local office of the U.S. Immigration and Naturalization Service must approve a request for permission to work. With this permission, work is authorized for a maximum of 20 hours per week while school is in session and full time during vacation periods. On-campus employment must be performed on the premises of the institution in which the student is enrolled, and such employment must not interfere with the student's ability to carry a full program of study. An F-1 student may be employed on campus without special authorization if awarded a scholarship, assistantship, or fellowship, since these are considered part of the student's program of study. If the job is unrelated to the student's course of study, the foreign student may not be employed if doing so would displace a U.S. worker. Dependents of F-1 students (spouse and unmarried minor children only) can be admitted to the United States on F-2 visas. They are admitted for the purpose of accompanying the F-1 student to the United States, and may not be authorized to accept employment under any circumstances.

The exchange-visitor sponsor or responsible officer at the sponsoring organization or institution has the authority to grant off-campus work permission to the J-1 student or scholar without referring the matter to the U.S. Immigration and Naturalization Service only if the sponsor determines that employment is necessary because of an "urgent financial need which has arisen since acquiring exchange visitor status" and will not cause the student to carry less that a full program of study. With this permission, work is authorized for a maximum of 20 hours per week while school is in session and full time during vacation periods. Regulations for J-1 students to be employed in on-campus positions are similar to those for F-1 students, with the additional requirement that permission for such employment must be granted by the exchange-program sponsor. Spouses and unmarried minor children of J-1 students can be admitted to the United States on J-2 visas. They may apply to the U.S. Immigration and Naturalization Service for permission to work for their own support, but not to support the exchange visitor. Each case is decided individually.

Applicants for U.S. visas must have a passport that is valid for at least six months longer than the intended stay in the United States. Their exit and reentry permits must be valid for at least six months beyond the date of the visa application. All applicants for U.S. visas are interviewed. Applicants should not go to the U.S. Embassy or consulates more than 60 days in advance of the date they are required to begin their studies in the United States. In Beijing, the Chinese government requires that applicants for U.S. visas present documents to the Chinese security officer stationed at the entrance to the embassy compound before they will be admitted to the embassy to apply for a visa. Privately sponsored students must submit their passport. Officially sponsored students must submit a note from the sponsoring ministry and their passport. (Work-unit permission is also required of students who are visiting China during a vacation period and need a new visa to reenter the United States.) The major hurdle in obtaining a visa is the requirement that applicants present compelling reasons for returning to China, not emigrating to the United States. Examples of these "compelling ties" are economic/employment, family position and tradition, and high status in China. English-language proficiency is another obvious requirement for being granted a visa.

At the present time, the U.S. government issues double-entry visas to Chinese students on F-1 visas that are valid for six months and to Chinese students and scholars on J-1 visas that are valid for six months. Negotiations currently are under way between the U.S. and Chinese governments to clarify the types of visas issued to Chinese and U.S. citizens. U.S. consular officers do not require two I-20s for individuals coming to the United States to study English as a second language; however, unless there is an indication that the student will be accepted into a regular academic program upon completion of English study, they might turn down a visa request for English study only. A U.S. visa will be issued to a J-1 visa applicant who does not speak English only when the receiving institution indicates in writing (on the Form IAP-66 or an attached sheet) that English proficiency is not required.

Once the visa application is submitted, the time required for processing is three to six working days. Each case is adjudicated on its own merits; except in special circumstances, the U.S. Embassy and consulates do not need to receive prior approval from the Department of State before issuing a visa. Students and scholars with a passport issued by the Ministry of Foreign Affairs who are visiting China during a vacation must present a note from the ministry before they will be granted a visa to reenter the United States.

To help prevent the late arrival on U.S. campuses of degree-seeking J-1 students, U.S. consular officials recommend U.S. institutions put a notation on the Form IAP-66 that states the latest acceptable arrival date. They also have indicated that if U.S. institutions wish to communicate with the U.S. Embassy in Beijing, telex communication is permitted in emergency situations; written correspondence, however, is preferred. Specific questions about visa matters can also be directed to Visa Services, Coordination Division, Department of State, CA/VO/L/C, 2401 E Street, N.W., Room 1343, Washington, DC 20520, phone: 202/663-1210.

Pre-Arrival Arrangements and Initial Concerns

Even though information about the United States has become more plentiful in China since 1978, many Chinese have little knowledge of day-to-day life in the United States or of life on U.S. college and university campuses. To alleviate this situation and assist Chinese students and scholars, the U.S.-China Education Clearinghouse has prepared a handbook of general orientation materials, *Bound for the United States: An Introduction to U.S. College and University Life*. The handbook was distributed in China by the U.S. government; copies should be available in the educational advising centers. The U.S. Information Agency has also produced a follow-up publication entitled *Pre-Departure Orientation Handbook: For Students from the People's Republic of China Planning to Study in the United States* that is available in the educational advising centers. However, orientation materials and instructions about arrival and settling-in procedures specific to the U.S. host institution and community should be sent to the Chinese student or scholar as soon as offers of admission have been accepted. Matters of concern to foreign student advisers and Chinese students and scholars are outlined below. For more detailed suggestions, the reader is referred to the U.S.-China Education Clearinghouse publication *Assisting Students and Scholars from the People's Republic of China: A Handbook for Community Groups*, which is available from NAFSA.

Many Chinese students and scholars travel to the United States on direct flights now available between Beijing or Shanghai and New York or San Francisco. Chinese-government-sponsored students may be met in San Francisco or New York by staff from the Chinese consulate, who will assist in making arrangements for the remainder of their trip. Final arrival notices may be phoned to the U.S. institution. However, because of delays in obtaining passports and visas in China or last-minute changes of plans, arrivals may occur with little advance warning. U.S. institutions should be prepared to cope with such situations. Also, Chinese custom leads newly arriving students and scholars to expect that they will be met upon arrival by a representative of the host institution.

Chinese students and scholars often anticipate that their U.S. host institution will resemble their home unit and expect that their new U.S. "unit" to provide the same kind of assistance. In receiving Chinese students and scholars on campus, U.S. institutions should be sensitive to this expectation, particularly with regard to such concerns as who will oversee and advise the academic program, who will arrange for housing, and who will arrange for medical care and insurance. Foreign student advisers should plan a thorough orientation to campus and community life for Chinese students and scholars; in many instances, Chinese students and scholars who have been on campus for awhile can assist in orienting their colleagues.

Some foreign student advisers have formed small working groups of people interested in China who are willing to assist with logistical problems, such as temporary housing. Students and scholars should be introduced to a variety of modestly priced options for permanent housing arrangements close to the campus or within easy commuting distance by public transportation or bicycle. (Dependents usually do not accompany Chinese students and scholars.) Explanations of items such as contracts and leases and apartment and utilities deposits, and information about safety of neighborhoods and other items related to locating appropriate permanent housing, should be included in orientation discussions, as these are unfamiliar to most Chinese students and scholars.

In addition to normal settling-in activities and adjustment to living in a new social environment, Chinese students and scholars may have language-related problems. Most officially sponsored students and scholars receive intensive English-language training prior to their departure from China, but they may still be unsure of their oral/aural skills—especially, as is usually the case, if their language training was received quite some time before their departure from China. Since the Chinese government seldom provides money for additional English-language training in the United States, they usually will welcome informal conversation and tutoring sessions organized by campus or community volunteers. Many Americans welcome opportunities to meet and talk with Chinese students and scholars. Foreign student advisers should help arrange formal and informal encounters between

Chinese and Americans, remembering that the Chinese will need time to adapt and may be reluctant to meet U.S. journalists in particular until long after their arrival in the United States.

Students and scholars from the People's Republic of China and Taiwan have generally been eager to meet one another on U.S. campuses, and have established cordial or even friendly working and social ties. It should be recognized, however, that the PRC's citizens are likely to be very sensitive to the use of the terms "Republic of China" or "Nationalist China" in reference to Taiwan, and attention should be given to how official records, reports, and other lists within the university describe their country of origin or nationality (see Chapter 13).

Having Chinese students and scholars on campus may prompt visits by U.S. government security agents. Such visits generally have been directed to foreign student advisers and faculty working with Chinese scholars.

Financial Matters

Stipends received by officially sponsored Chinese students and scholars currently vary between $380 and $440 per month. A number of U.S. institutions have expressed concern about this low level, particularly in regard to the cost of living, the cost of medical insurance, and the need to cover such additional expenses as travel to professional meetings that may be an important part of the student's or scholar's academic program. Some U.S. institutions have supplemented the stipend received from the Chinese government; others have begun to require higher stipend levels as a condition of acceptance. The responsible officer of an exchange visitor program has the obligation to ensure that stipends agreed to prior to acceptance are in fact being provided.

The stipend payments of officially sponsored Chinese students and scholars are processed by the Chinese Embassy in Washington, DC, or by one of the Chinese consulates located in Chicago, Houston, New York, and San Francisco. Stipends are sent to most Chinese students and scholars once every three months. Individuals sponsored by the Chinese government for a brief stay in the United States probably will receive their living stipend for the entire length of their visit upon arrival in the United States. Any questions regarding the schedule of remittance or adequacy of stipends should be addressed to the education section of the Chinese Embassy or appropriate Chinese consulate. (See Appendix H for addresses and phone numbers.)

Insurance and Medical Care

Medical expenses in China are very low, and most Chinese students and scholars find it difficult to comprehend just how expensive medical care can be in the United States and how important it is to have adequate medical insurance. Since medical costs would normally be covered by their home institutions in China, many assume that they are automatically insured by their new "unit" and do not understand the need to pay for coverage or care beyond that provided by campus clinics. Moreover, since medical insurance usually covers only part of the cost of medical care, Chinese students and scholars may be concerned when they learn that most policies do not cover all costs.

In June 1986, the Embassy of the People's Republic of China signed an agreement with the Penteco Insurance Company for an insurance policy underwritten by the Delaware American Life Insurance Company to cover Chinese students and scholars in the United States. That policy still is in effect. The policy was established specifically for Chinese-government-sponsored students and scholars, but any Chinese student and scholar in the United States may subscribe to it. Chinese-government-sponsored students and scholars are required to subscribe to the Penteco policy, with two exceptions: (1) if the U.S. institution requires all foreign students to purchase the institution's own insurance or (2) if the U.S. institution's insurance policy is more comprehensive and provides better coverage. Chinese students and scholars who are privately sponsored are permitted to purchase any insurance they wish—either from the institution or Penteco, or any other coverage.

For the 1987–88 academic year, the fee for the Penteco policy was $25 per month for students and scholars, $38 per month for spouses, and $32 per month for children. Students and scholars pay the monthly fee on a semi-annual basis directly to the insurance company. Information available to the embassy indicates that, to date, payments have been made in a timely fashion by students and scholars. Information about the Penteco policy is sent each year to all officially sponsored students and scholars in the United States. Persons who have not received information directly should contact the Chinese Embassy in Washington or Penteco, Inc., 1001 Connecticut Avenue, N.W., Washington, DC 20036, phone: 800/722-0086 or 202/347-7324.

U.S. institutions should specify the amount of insurance costs on the Certificate of Eligibility or in the accompanying letter so sponsors will realize that funds to cover these expenses must be provided.

CHINEX Students and Scholars

Many visas for Chinese students and scholars are stamped with the symbol "212(d)(3)(A)(28)." This indicates that the bearer requires special permission to enter the United States. Some of the visas have the additional notation "CHINEX." This is a designation similar to "SPLEX," which is used for students from the Soviet Union and Eastern European countries. It refers to inclusion under the educational exchange agreement between the United States and the People's Republic of China. A CHINEX student or scholar is defined as any citizen of the People's Republic of China visiting the United States to participate in an exchange-visitor program financed by the U.S. or Chinese government and/or to lecture, perform research, or study in a scientific or technical field. The CHINEX designation may appear on either J-1 or F-1 visas.

Until February 1, 1985, CHINEX students and scholars were subject to access controls. These controls required them to notify the State Department in writing whenever professional travel was planned. Professional travel was any travel outside the host institution related to the visitor's academic work, such as travel to a conference, laboratory, research facility, or factory. Travel restrictions were imposed by the Department of State in response to similar controls placed on U.S. students and scholars in China. In addition to travel restrictions, the Department of State required clearance for a CHINEX student or scholar to extend his or her stay in the United States and/or to transfer between institutions. With the February 1, 1985 changes, CHINEX students and scholars are subject to the same body of regulations which apply to all J-1 exchange visitors. Further restrictions continue to apply to those Chinese nationals whose visas contain the notation 212(d)(3)(A)(28), however (see below).

Travel Outside the United States

Many Chinese students and scholars arrange to travel to other countries during their stay in the United States. Before departing, the visitors should ensure that their papers are in order for reentry to the United States. Since Chinese students and scholars receive six-month double-entry visas, they will usually need to renew their visas while they are abroad. An exception to this requirement is when they travel to Canada, Mexico, or an adjacent island. If Chinese students and scholars do not have the 212(d)(3)(A)(28) notation on their visas and wish to travel to Canada, Mexico, or an adjacent island for less than 30 days, they need not obtain a new visa to reenter the United States. The

Immigration and Naturalization Service will automatically revalidate an expired nonimmigrant visa of a foreign national whose temporary absence from the United States of not more than 30 days has been "solely in contiguous territory or adjacent islands other than Cuba" (that is, Canada, Mexico, or Caribbean islands other than Cuba). Chinese nationals should not relinquish the Form I-94 (Arrival/Departure Record) when departing from the United States, and they should be certain to carry with them their passport and valid Form IAP-66 or I-20 and I-20ID.

If Chinese students and scholars do have the 212(d)(3)(A)(28) notation on their visas and wish to travel to Canada, Mexico, or an adjacent island for less than 30 days, the foreign student adviser should request pre-authorization from the Visa Office. This request must come from the foreign student adviser, not the student or scholar who wishes to travel. A copy of the pre-authorization request form is contained in Appendix I.

The following information is required by the Visa Office about the Chinese student or scholar:

- name
- sex
- date of birth
- place of birth
- occupation in China
- employer in China
- purpose of visit to the foreign country
- date of departure from the United States
- date of return to the United States
- U.S. Embassy or consulate in the foreign country where the applicant will apply for a new U.S. visa
- address in the United States of the foreign embassy or consulate where the Chinese national will be applying for a visa
- the length of stay in the United States of the student or scholar upon return.

The form must be accompanied by photocopies of the expired U.S. visa, the Form I-94, and the Form IAP-66 or I-20A, as well as a letter, when appropriate, from the U.S. institution. The form and accompanying documents should be sent to Visa Services, Coordination Division, Department of State, CA/VO/L/C, 2401 E Street, N.W., Room 1343, Washington, DC 20520.

The U.S. Embassy and consulates in China will process the visa application for any Chinese national traveling home for a vacation or an extended period of time without prior referral to the Visa Office, providing the student or scholar possesses a valid Form IAP-66 or I-20, a valid passport, and an official letter from either the department head or foreign student adviser that the applicant is expected back at the institution. The Visa Office helps to facilitate the re-issuance of visas to all nationals of the People's Republic of China who wish to leave the United States to travel to a third country for a very brief period to participate in a seminar or conference, a third country for a short period as a member of a tour group, or China for a verifiable family emergency.

If any Chinese national wishes to make a brief trip to a third country that is not a continguous territory or adjacent island, the diplomatic mission of that country may require a letter from the Department of State before processing the Chinese citizen's visa. The U.S. embassy or consulate in the country to be visited also needs to be notified so it can process the Chinese national's visa expeditiously. In these cases, the procedures to be followed are:

1. The foreign student adviser should notify the Department of State of the Chinese student's or scholar's travel plans by completing a pre-authorization request form (sample in Appendix I) with the information noted above and sending it and the required accompanying documents as noted above to Visa Services, Coordination Division, Department of State, CA/VO/L/C, 2401 E Street, N.W., Room 1343, Washington, DC 20520.

2. The Visa Office will then send letters to the appropriate foreign embassy or consulate in the United States and the U.S. Embassy or consulate in the country to be visited stating that the Chinese visitor has authorization to travel to the country from which the visa is being requested and to reenter the United States.

3. The Chinese student or scholar should apply to the appropriate foreign embassy or consulate in the United States for a visa.

4. When the Chinese student or scholar reapplies for his or her visa at the U.S. Embassy or consulate abroad for reentry into the United States, he or she must present a valid passport, two passport photographs, a copy of the valid IAP-66 or I-20, and the visa application.

This procedure does not guarantee visa issuance. This service can only be undertaken if special regulations regarding visa issuance, which apply to many applicants, are not in effect. This procedure is only an assurance to the consular officer at the post where the applicant is to apply that certain aspects of the visa issuance procedure have been completed. Every nonimmigrant visa applicant must demonstrate at the time of application that he or she qualifies in all respects for the type visa he or she seeks or the visa cannot be issued.

Extensions of Stay

Chinese students who wish to apply for extensions of stay must receive permission from their work units in China to do so. Students on J-1 visas also should receive permission from the Chinese Embassy or consulates. (In the fall of 1987, representatives of the Education Division of the Chinese Embassy reported that approximately 50 percent of students on J-1 visas wishing extensions are requesting permission from the Chinese Embassy or consulates in addition to their work units.) It is the responsibility of the student, not the foreign student adviser, to apply for the needed permission. Once this permission has been granted, Chinese students, as do all other nationalities, must request a new IAP-66 from the exchange-visitor program's responsible officer in order to extend their stay.

A change in regulations for extensions of stay for Chinese scholars was mandated by the Chinese government on April 11, 1987. Scholars sponsored by the Chinese government are permitted to stay in the United States for three months to one year with government funding. They may have a maximum extension of six months if they obtain funding from another source and receive permission from their work unit.

Change of J-1 Category

During the early years of U.S.-China educational exchanges, the U.S. government's policy prohibiting a change of J-1 category from scholar to student was not normally applied to scholars from the People's Republic of China. The U.S. Information Agency (USIA) basically made this exception because of the lack of familiarity of U.S. institutions with the Chinese education system and the resultant difficulty in assessing Chinese academic credentials. In 1986, however, USIA revised this practice. The decision was based on two factors. First, it was believed that there existed in the United States a sufficient body of knowledge about the Chinese education system to enable decisions to be made about the appropriate admittance status of a Chinese applicant prior to his or her arrival in the United States. Second, Chinese-government representatives requested the assistance of USIA in preventing Chinese-government-sponsored scholars from delaying their return to China after they had completed their initial educational program in the United States. (A change in category almost always included an additional period of stay in the United States beyond the initial program.) Thus, on June 30, 1987, the agreement that existed between the U.S. and Chinese governments allowing a possible change of J-1 category from scholar to student for Chinese nationals ended. Now, Chinese citizens are subject to the same regulations as are all other foreign nationals; any Chinese citizen coming to the United States as a scholar is not permitted to change category to a student by either the Chinese government or USIA.

The Chinese government instituted the following regulations for Chinese scholars who had come to the United States prior to January 1, 1987:

1. To obtain a change of category, scholars had to have requested permission from their work unit in China; the work unit, if other than the State Education Commission, had to have requested permission from the State Education Commission to grant the scholar's request. The State Education Commission, if approving the request, then sent approval to the Chinese Embassy in Washington, DC; the Chinese Embassy sent a letter of permission to USIA, which began to consider the request. This procedure was applicable to all persons on J-1 visas, whether sponsored by the Chinese government or privately sponsored. USIA would only accept letters of permission from the Chinese Embassy, not from any of the Chinese consulates in the United States. When USIA received the request from the Chinese Embassy, it began to consider it, but that did not mean that it would be automatically approved.

2. The Chinese government did not encourage persons over 35 years of age to pursue graduate studies.

3. If a scholar under 35 years of age wished to change category to that of a student, he or she had to have made the request during the first year of stay in the United States and not have waited until the end of the period as a scholar.

4. If a scholar decided in the first year in the United States that he or she wished to change category to a student, he or she must have received financial support from the U.S. institution and then reported this to the Chinese Embassy and the work unit in China.

5. The Chinese Embassy established a deadline of April 30, 1987 for the submission of requests for a change of category. However, if the request for a change of category had been submitted to the work unit in China prior to April 30, 1987 but had not reached the embassy by that date, the application still would be processed. Requests for changes of category that had not been initiated prior to April 30, 1987 would only be considered if the applicant could show very special reasons why a change was necessary.

Since the special conditions extended to Chinese scholars on J-1 visas have ended, and since this fact may not be known to all personnel at U.S. institutions, foreign student advisers should address the desire of a Chinese scholar to change status to that of student in the following manner. When a request is received from a faculty member to issue a Form IAP-66 to a Chinese citizen to come to the United States as a scholar, the foreign student adviser should contact the faculty member to make certain the Chinese applicant does not in fact wish to be a student, explaining that if the person enters the United States as a scholar, he or she will not under any circumstances be able to change category to a student while in the United States.

Change of Institution

Since restrictions affecting CHINEX students and scholars wishing to change institutions have been rescinded, all Chinese students and scholars who wish to change institutions now follow the same procedures as do other foreign nationals.

U.S. Income Tax Liability and Social Security

The U.S. Senate ratified the U.S. Tax Agreement with the People's Republic of China on July 24, 1986, more than two years after President Reagan and Premier Zhao Ziyang signed the treaty in Beijing. It is effective for tax years beginning on or after January 1, 1987. Among the treaty's sections are provisions providing tax relief to both Chinese students and scholars in the United States and U.S. students and scholars in China.

The treaty is intended to prevent double taxation; but with regard to the U.S. tax code, the treaty also appears to provide some relief to Chinese students and scholars receiving scholarships. Article 19 of the treaty allows nonimmigrant Chinese teachers and researchers in the United States to exclude "remuneration for . . . teaching, lectures, or research" from U.S. income tax for up to an aggregate of three years. Article 20 allows a nonimmigrant Chinese student or trainee in the United States to exclude "payments from abroad for the purpose of his or her maintenance, education, study, research, or training" from U.S. income tax. In addition, grants and awards (if from a government, scientific, educational, or other tax-exempt organization) and income from personal services, up to $5,000 per year, are excluded from U.S. income tax. These two articles extend similar treatment to U.S. residents in China. Relief from double taxation for U.S. residents is provided through a tax credit, which is described in Article 22 of the treaty. A Department of Treasury official has stated that its provisions take precedence over any conflicting sections of the new tax code passed by Congress in the fall of 1986.

Persons on F-1 or J-1 visas are not required to pay social security or unemployment taxes. They should examine their first pay check to make certain the employer is not deducting these taxes. If these taxes are being deducted, the employer should be referred to IRS Circular E No. 15, "Employers' Tax Guide," which gives tax information for nonresident aliens. This circular is available in local IRS distribution offices or by calling 800/424-FORMS.

Accompanying Family Members

According to regulations issued by the Chinese government in December 1986, family members are not allowed to join students pursuing graduate studies overseas for periods of less than three years. Students planning overseas graduate study for periods of more than three years are permitted to take their families with them.

If spouses of Chinese students in the United States wish to come for a visit, they may receive three months' paid vacation from their work unit to do so. They may remain in the United States for an additional three months with the permission of the work unit without receiving any pay. If they remain in the United States longer than six months, they are no longer considered a member of their work unit in China. However, if a spouse is admitted to a U.S. institution during the stay in the United States, receives funding from that institution, and is issued an I-20 or IAP-66 by the institution, the spouse can receive permission from the work unit to remain in the United States to attend school.

In China, spouses who are separated because of job assignments for one year are given 20 days vacation to spend together. However, since Chinese scholars are expected to be in the United States for no longer than one year, their spouses are not encouraged to visit them. Even if a scholar extends his or her stay in the United States for an additional six months, the spouse is not encouraged to come for a visit. Husbands and wives are allowed to come to the United States together if both have been accepted by U.S. institutions as scholars or students.

Residency Requirements for Holders of J-1 Visas

As with all other foreign students and scholars, Chinese nationals in the United States on J-1 visas who are funded by their home government or the U.S. government or whose major profession is included on the Exchange Visitors Skills List are subject to the two-year home-residency requirement: they must reside in China for two years after completion of their academic program. The People's Republic of China was included for the first time on the Exchange Visitor Skills List published on June 6, 1984. The number of groups of designated fields of specialized knowledge or skills included for the PRC is extensive. Persons wishing a copy of the Exchange Visitor Skills List should contact the Exchange Visitor Facilitative Service Staff, Office of the General Counsel and Congressional Liaison, U.S. Information Agency, 301 4th Street, S.W., Room 700, Washington, DC 20547, phone: 202/485-7976.

To determine whether a Chinese student who arrived in the United States prior to the issuance of the skills list in 1984 is subject to the two-year home-residency requirement, foreign student advisers should either check the pink copy of the IAP-66 to determine sponsorship or check the student's passport to identify the issuing agency. If the passport was issued by the Foreign Affairs Ministry or a provincial foreign affairs office, it indicates that the student was sponsored by the government, even if the government only paid for transportation. The student is therefore subject to the two-year home-residency requirement. If the passport was issued by the Public Security Bureau, the student was privately sponsored and is not subject to the two-year home-residency requirement.

Waivers of the two-year home-residency requirement can be obtained only in one of the following manners: (1) a letter of no objection is submitted by the home government; (2) a U.S. government agency submits a letter stating that the individual is needed by that agency in the United States; (3) there is a fear of persecution if the individual returns to his or her home country; or (4) the return of the foreign national to his or her home country will cause a severe hardship to a U.S. citizen, permanent resident spouse, or child. None of these exceptions is available to doctors or nurses.

15
U.S.-Chinese Institutional Arrangements

Summary of Current Arrangements

A number of U.S. and Chinese academic institutions have signed formal agreements to facilitate the exchange of students, researchers, and faculty. These agreements encompass a variety of forms and provisions. Some establish formal "sister institution" relationships, although it is not altogether clear what this means or how such relationships differ from other institution-to-institution ties. Others obligate the U.S. institution to receive a specific number of students and/or scholars from the partner institution annually, or to send a designated number of students and faculty to the Chinese counterpart each year. Still others obligate the U.S. or Chinese institution to provide a certain number of scholarships, fellowships, or stipends at levels from undergraduate students through faculty. Some institution-to-institution agreements cover exchanges only in selected academic fields.

Available data indicate that the number of Chinese students and scholars coming to the United States and Americans going to China under formal exchange agreements is small in comparison with the overall totals. However, a high percentage of individuals exchanged under formal agreements attend prestigious institutions in the receiving country.

Some U.S. institutions have decided not to negotiate formal exchange agreements with Chinese counterparts, preferring to work through informal arrangements. Available data are inadequate to draw firm conclusions about the effects of formal agreements on U.S.-Chinese educational exchanges, but many of the U.S. institutions reporting the largest population of Chinese students and scholars on campus do have formal exchange agreements with Chinese institutions.

For more detailed information about U.S.-China institutional arrangements, readers are referred to the U.S.-China Education

Clearinghouse publication *Students and Scholars from the People's Republic of China in the United States, August 1981: A Survey Summary,* which is available from NAFSA, and the National Academy Press's *A Relationship Restored: Trends in U.S.-China Educational Exchanges, 1978–1984.*

Guidelines for Establishing Special Relationships

A U.S. institution wishing to establish either formal or informal arrangements with a Chinese counterpart should realize that differences in the education systems of the United States and China, the absence of communication between the two countries for 30 years, and Chinese constraints on funding, living accommodations, and access to research materials can create difficulties and misunderstandings. In negotiating agreements, Americans must recall the highly specialized nature of most Chinese institutions (see Part One). Because of this, it may be desirable or necessary to develop ties with several Chinese institutions or between a specific U.S. department and a Chinese college (e.g., between a U.S. aeronautical engineering department and a Chinese aeronautical engineering college, or between a U.S. electrical engineering department and a Chinese radio engineering college). Names of Chinese institutions can be misleading, and it is important to examine curricula closely before proceeding with an agreement.

Initial contacts can be made by mail, but face-to-face communication with Chinese academic administrators is critical to establishing sound ties. It is also an important courtesy to keep the Chinese Embassy in Washington, DC, informed of negotiations. U.S. institutions may wish to invite Chinese educators to the United States, which would normally involve paying all in-country costs but not international travel, or to send a representative group to China. In the latter case, one can either offer to pay all in-China expenses or call for an exchange of delegations in which in-country costs are borne by the host institutions.

U.S. negotiators must be aware of the intent and limitations of the U.S. institution in discussing visits by Chinese to the United States. As no U.S. policy sets the parameters for educational exchange agreements, individual colleges and universities must decide what types of exchanges (age, group, fields, qualifications) they want to foster. They must also decide how many Chinese to receive, and on what terms (status designation, fee structure, duration of stay). This "package" should be presented to the Chinese in explicit terms to avoid misunderstanding. In addition to carefully outlining the levels and specific fields of study of students and/or scholars, the U.S. institution should specify clearly all financial arrangements, such as who will pay for international travel, tuition (if relevant), living stipends (and at what level), insurance costs, and lab fees.

Americans going to China to conduct research should request detailed information about which departments and research topics are open to foreigners. Past misunderstandings on this point have created difficult situations and animosity between Chinese administrators and U.S. students and researchers. Detailed information about available accommodations for Americans in China should also be obtained in advance, since housing shortages constitute a major problem in the PRC. This also raises the question whether the Americans-to-China part of the program should be established on a sending-side-pays or a hosting-side-pays basis. If the host side pays, China can cover only moderate room and board expenses for Americans in China, so recipients must also secure support from U.S. sources. Conversely, if the sending side pays, the costs for Americans in China can be extremely high: room and board in tourist accommodations can cost more than $1,000 per month.

16
Opportunities for Study, Research, and Teaching in China

The normalization of relations between the United States and China has allowed many Americans to travel to the PRC as tourists, students, researchers, or teachers. Package tours exist for individuals wishing to travel to China for short periods of time. Some are arranged by airlines or steamship companies; others, designed for special interest groups with a professional focus, are sponsored by several of the U.S. organizations listed in Appendix J. Detailed information about academic life in China appears in the National Academy Press publication *China Bound: A Guide to Academic Life and Work in the PRC*. The major opportunities for persons wishing to go to China to study, conduct research, or teach are discussed briefly below.

Study and Research

The Committee on Scholarly Communication with the People's Republic of China administers the major nationwide student and scholar exchange programs between the United States and China, including the National Program for Advanced Study and Research in China and the Visiting Scholar Exchange Program. For more information about these programs, write to the Committee on Scholarly Communication with the People's Republic of China, 2101 Constitution Avenue, N.W., Washington, DC 20418. A limited number of Fulbright awards are available for study and research in China. For further information, contact the International Education Program, U.S. Department of Education, Washington, DC 20202.

Many U.S. colleges and universities have formal or informal exchange agreements with Chinese institutions for short- or long-term programs. A list of schools known to have formal exchange agreements is included in *China Bound: A Guide to Academic Life and Work in the PRC*. Many programs are limited to students and faculty at the signatory institution, but questions of eligibility should be directed to the individual college or university. In addition to exchange programs conducted under agreements between U.S. and Chinese institutions, a number of summer and/or semester or year-long Chinese-language programs exist, as do other short-term programs (some with courses taught in English). These may be sponsored by individual U.S. institutions or by organizations such as the Council on International Educational Exchange, 205 East 42nd Street, New York, NY 10017. Information about these programs should be available in the study abroad office at most U.S. colleges and universities.

Individuals wishing to study or conduct research in China may also apply directly to the State Education Commission of China. Procedures and other pertinent information about this option are included in *China Bound: A Guide to Academic Life and Work in the PRC*. A copy of "A List of Specialities in Chinese Universities and Colleges Open to Foreign Students" can be obtained from NAFSA.

Teaching

For the first several years after normalization of relations between the United States and the People's Republic of China, the Chinese Foreign Experts Bureau (FEB) was responsible for the recruitment policy and day-to-day administration of programs for foreigners going to China to teach at institutions of higher education. As of 1988, the Foreign Experts Bureau, which now reports directly to the State Council, continues to be responsible for overall policy concerning foreigners teaching in China. Recruiting and administration, however, are now carried out by various agencies and institutions, depending on whether an individual is considered a "foreign expert" or a "foreign teacher." Detailed descriptions of the distinctions in qualifications, salaries, and benefits between foreign experts and foreign teachers are included in *China Bound: A Guide to Academic Life and Work in the PRC*. Information about the recruitment of foreign experts and foreign teachers is briefly described below.

Foreign Experts. The Foreign Experts Bureau only recruits foreign experts for smaller universities that are not under the authorization of the State Education Commission. In addition, it recruits English language specialists to train young interpreters and to write articles for the *Xinhua* News Agency, *Beijing Review*, *China Reconstructs*, and other English-language publications produced in China. The Bureau of Foreign Affairs of the State Education Commission is responsible for recruiting foreign experts for all other universities and for overseeing their stay in China. The regulations outlined in the FEB's 1985 brochure *Information on the Recruitment of Foreign Experts* apply to all foreign experts traveling to China. The brochure, including an application form and a health certificate, is included in *China Bound: A Guide to Academic Life and Work in the PRC*. Applications should be sent to the Foreign Experts Bureau of the State Council, P.O. Box 300, Beijing, People's Republic of China.

Foreign Teachers. Foreign teachers are recruited directly by Chinese institutions of higher learning, university departments, or local provincial or municipal departments or bureaus of education. Applications for these teaching positions should be sent directly to the interested office.

Several agencies and institutions recruit both foreign experts and foreign teachers. When applying for teaching positions, inquire whether the position is that of a foreign expert or foreign teacher and what the conditions of employment are.

Personnel at the Education Division of the Chinese Embassy in Washington recruit U.S. educators and professionals to work in China. They are specifically interested in lecturers and professors to teach English, science and technology, finance, banking, business management, and law in Chinese institutions of higher education. They also recruit individuals for editing, translating, and publishing positions with the press, radio, and publishing houses. Personnel selected to teach in China are expected to perform the following assignments:

- upgrade the professional skills of Chinese foreign-language teachers
- teach both undergraduate and graduate students
- counsel and guide Chinese teachers
- offer advice on extracurricular language-training activities and supervise graduate students in writing academic papers
- compile and edit teaching and reference materials
- give lectures about the United States on such topics as culture, history, or other subjects as required.

Applicants must hold a master's or higher degree, demonstrate relatively high attainment in their own field, and have some teaching or work experience, preferably for at least three years. Persons who wish to apply for a teaching position in China should send an application and health certificate, a detailed resume, and two letters of recommendation to the Education Division, Embassy of the People's Republic of China, 2300 Connecticut Avenue, N.W., Washington, DC 20008.

A number of other organizations and institutions in the United

States recruit individuals to teach in China. A limited number of Fulbright awards are available for teaching in China. (For further information, write to the Council for International Exchange of Scholars, 11 Dupont Circle, N.W., Suite 300, Washington, DC 20036.) Americans who wish to teach in China should also contact the appropriate office at their home institution to see whether a formal or informal agreement exists between their institution and one in China that includes the exchange of faculty. If individuals have personal friends at specific Chinese institutions or have met Chinese scholars visiting the United States, they also can write directly to those individuals or institutions requesting information about teaching opportunities.

PART FOUR

The Future of U.S.-China Educational Exchanges

Progress in educational exchanges between the United States and the People's Republic of China has been extraordinary; few people nine years ago would have predicted the extent of their success. Many benefits have already been realized by both sides. Nevertheless, problems remain, as they must in any new venture that has developed as rapidly as this one. Some problems are procedural or mechanical. Much progress has been made in resolving these, and in ameliorating other weaknesses in the exchange process—such as the insufficiency of counseling provided to Chinese students and scholars wishing to come to the United States, the inability of all students who wish to take U.S. standardized admissions tests to do so, the level of financial support provided by the Chinese government or other sources, and the lack of information about some Chinese institutions of higher education. These difficulties can be expected to be resolved over time.

One of the clearest indications that such problems will be resolved is the continued importance being placed on international educational exchanges by the State Education Commission. Representatives of the commission have been extremely pragmatic in facilitating exchanges with the United States. For example, their decision to administer U.S. standardized admissions tests in China reflected an awareness that U.S. institutions could not continue indefinitely the temporary measures and waivers of certain requirements necessary to initiate exchanges with China. They realized that unless it became easier for Chinese applicants to conform to "normal" requirements and procedures, the applicants would not be able to compete successfully for admission or financial aid.

Other problems that are somewhat different and perhaps less easily resolved include varying perceptions of the meaning of "reciprocity," the United States' interest in access to Chinese scholarly materials and field sites, and the implementation of institution-to-institution agreements. The issue of "reciprocity," which is extraordinarily complex, reflects fundamentally different perceptions in each country. Americans believe U.S. students and scholars studying or conducting research in China should be treated in the same way as are Chinese nationals on U.S. campuses. This would give a student access to all departments and courses for which he or she has met necessary academic prerequisites, as well as full support and encouragement for independent research projects. The Chinese position is that just as Chinese nationals in the United States are treated the same as all other foreign students, Americans on PRC campuses should be—and are—treated the same as all other foreign students in China. The relevant standard of comparison, they argue, is not what is done in the United States, but what is done in China with respect to other foreign students and scholars. The major difference is the amount of freedom that all students, American and foreign, are given on U.S. campuses and the restrictions placed upon all foreign students in China.

The issue of access to materials and facilities is closely linked to this issue of reciprocity. Chinese students and scholars on U.S. campuses enjoy the same access to library collections, computer and photocopy facilities, laboratories, and other facilities as do U.S. students and faculty. That is not always the case in China. Certain library collections, card catalogs, reference materials, and other facilities essential for the efficient conduct of research are off limits to foreigners—and frequently to Chinese scholars as well—in China. Limitations on the ability of U.S. students and scholars to conduct field research is also a difficult problem. For China specialists and social scientists/humanists generally, one of the most exciting aspects about the restoration of educational exchanges with China is the opportunity to gain access to otherwise unavailable archives, individuals, and field data. For a variety of reasons, it has proven difficult to realize the potential for conducting such research. Progress has been made on resolving the problems of both access to materials and facilities and conducting field research, and much more is possible now than was the case five years ago; still, problems remain to be resolved.

A different set of problems relates to the appropriateness of institution-to-institution agreements. Commitments to send and/or receive specified numbers of students and/or faculty are at the heart of most of the agreements concluded between U.S. and Chinese institutions. Although the total number of persons to be exchanged is generally quite small (on the order of two to ten per year), the U.S. institution often cannot find enough American students and/or faculty willing and qualified to spend one year at the Chinese partner institution. The number of U.S. students whose mastery of the Chinese language would allow them to attend regular courses in China is very small; those with sufficient language competence are often advanced graduate students who desire to conduct research rather than attend classes. The specialized interest of advanced graduate students and faculty might make it more appropriate for them to spend their time in China at an institution other than the partner school of their home university. In order to fill the number of slots specified in agreements, U.S. institutions have sometimes sent abroad students who were not adequately prepared for regular classes at a Chinese university. This has caused enormous difficulties for the partner institution, because few PRC institutions are prepared to receive foreign students with severe language deficiencies. Additionally, students who have been sent to Chinese colleges under institution-to-institution arrangements sometimes discover they cannot do the work they had envisioned because appropriate course offerings or research materials simply are not available at that institution.

Problems exist with exchanges at the national level, also. Recent years have witnessed a dramatic decline in the number of U.S. students in China-studies programs and in the number of good applicants for national exchange programs with China. In addition, financial problems have beset Americans who wish to study in China on one of the long- or short-term programs sponsored at the national level that do not provide funding. The number of Americans participating in exchanges with China is thus decreasing while the number of Chinese applicants to U.S. institutions greatly increases.

Many educators in both the United States and China who are seeking to resolve these problems believe the benefits of the exchanges far outweigh the disadvantages. They see the need to broaden horizons in thinking about the exchanges—for example, by linking episodic events and training to accomplish more truly collaborative work—and are encouraging colleagues to consider new options. Such new activities will assure that both countries are prepared to meet the continuing challenges of educational exchanges.

Appendices

Appendix A

Agreement Between
the Government of the United States of America
and
the Government of the People's Republic of China
on Cooperation in Science and Technology
January 31, 1979

The Government of the United States of America and the Government of the People's Republic of China (hereinafter referred to as the Contracting Parties);

Acting in the spirit of the Joint Communique on the Establishment of Diplomatic Relations between the United States of America and the People's Republic of China;

Recognizing that cooperation in the fields of science and technology can promote the well-being and prosperity of both countries;

Affirming that such cooperation can strengthen friendly relations between both countries;

Wishing to establish closer and more regular cooperation between scientific and technical entities and personnel in both countries;

Have agreed as follows:

Article 1

1. The Contracting Parties shall develop cooperation under this Agreement on the basis of equality, reciprocity and mutual benefit.

2. The principal objective of this Agreement is to provide broad opportunities for cooperation in scientific and technological fields of mutual interest, thereby promoting the progress of science and technology for the benefit of both countries and of mankind.

Article 2

Cooperation under this Agreement may be undertaken in the fields of agriculture, energy, space, health, environment, earth sciences, engineering, and such other areas of science and technology and their management as may be mutually agreed, as well as educational and scholarly exchange.

Article 3

Cooperation under this Agreement may include:

a. Exchange of scientists, scholars, specialists, and students;
b. Exchange of scientific, scholarly and technological information, and documentation;
c. Joint planning and implementation of programs and projects;
d. Joint research, development and testing, and exchange of research results and experience between cooperating entities;
e. Organization of joint courses, conferences, and symposia;
f. Other forms of scientific and technological cooperation as may be mutually agreed.

Article 4

Pursuant to the objectives of this Agreement, the Contracting Parties shall encourage and facilitate, as appropriate, the development of contacts and cooperation between government agencies, universities, organizations, institutions, and other entities of both countries, and the conclusion of accords between such bodies for the conduct of cooperative activities. Both sides will further promote, consistent with such cooperation and where appropriate, mutually beneficial bilateral economic activities.

Article 5

Specific accords implementing this Agreement may cover the subjects of cooperation, procedures to be followed, treatment of intellectual property, funding, and other appropriate matters. With respect to funding, costs shall be borne as mutually agreed. All cooperative activities under this Agreement shall be subject to the availability of funds.

Article 6

Cooperative activities under this Agreement shall be subject to the laws and regulations in each country.

Article 7

Each Contracting Party shall, with respect to cooperative activities under this Agreement, use its best efforts to facilitate prompt entry into and exit from its territory of equipment and personnel of the other side, and also to provide access to relevant geographic areas, institutions, data, and materials.

Article 8

Scientific and technological information derived from cooperative activities under this Agreement may be made available, unless otherwise agreed in an implementing accord under Article 5, to the world scientific community through customary channels and in accordance with the normal procedures of the participating entities.

Article 9

Scientists, technical experts, and entities of third countries or international organizations may be invited, upon mutual consent of both sides, to participate in projects and programs being carried out under this Agreement.

Article 10

1. The Contracting Parties shall establish a US-PRC Joint Commission on Scientific and Technological Cooperation, which shall consist of United States and Chinese parts. Each Contracting Party shall designate a co-chairman and its members of the Commission. The Commission shall adopt procedures for its operation, and shall ordinarily meet once a year in the United States and the People's Republic of China alternately.

2. The Joint Commission shall plan and coordinate cooperation in science and technology, and monitor and facilitate such cooperation. The Commission shall also consider proposals for the further development of cooperative activities in specific areas and recommend measures and programs to both sides.

3. To carry out its functions, the Commission may when necessary create temporary or permanent joint subcommittees or working groups.

4. During the period between meetings of the Commission, additions or amendments may be made to already approved cooperative activities, as may be mutually agreed.

5. To assist the Joint Commission, each Contracting Party shall designate an Executive Agent. The Executive Agent on the United States side shall be the Office of Science and Technology Policy; and on the side of the People's Republic of China, the State Scientific and Technological Commission. The Executive Agents shall collaborate closely to promote proper implementation of all activities and programs. The Executive Agent of each Contracting Party shall be responsible for coordinating the implementation of its side of such activities and programs.

Article 11

1. This Agreement shall enter into force upon signature and shall remain in force for five years. It may be modified or extended by mutual agreement of the Parties.

2. The termination of this Agreement shall not affect the validity or duration of any implmenting accords made under it.

Done at Washington this 31st day of January 1979 in duplicate in the English and Chinese languages, both equally authentic.

<table>
<tr><td>For the Government
of the
United States of America:</td><td>For the Government
of the
People's Republic of China:</td></tr>
<tr><td>JIMMY CARTER</td><td>DENG XIAOPING</td></tr>
</table>

Appendix B

Protocol Between
the Government of the United States of America
and the Government of the People's Republic of China
for Cooperation in Educational Exchanges
July 23, 1985

The Government of the United States of America and the Government of the People's Republic of China, represented by the United States Information Agency and the State Education Commission of the People's Republic of China, hereinafter referred to as "the Parties," recognizing the role of education in furthering progress in both nations and in building understanding between the people of the two countries, subject to the "Agreement on Cooperation in Science and Technology between the Government of the United States of America and the Government of the People's Republic of China" and in accordance with the principles of the "Cultural Agreement between the Government of the United States of America and the Government of the People's Republic of China," have, with a view to promoting educational exchanges, agreed on activities of educational exchanges described in this accord.

Article I — Guiding Principles

The Parties shall agree and affirm that the principal objective of this accord is to provide opportunities for cooperation and exchange in educational fields based on equality, reciprocity, and mutual benefit. Recognizing differences in the societies and systems of the two countries, both Parties will initiate educational exchange activities based on their own as well as mutual interests. The receiving side will facilitate and assist in implementing those educational exchange projects to every extent possible to assure that the requests of the sending side for study and research opportunities are met to the extent required in each case in accordance with each country's laws and regulations.

Both Parties will undertake measures to enhance educational exchange objectives. Scholarly data and information derived from activities under this accord may be made available to the world scholarly community through customary channels in accordance with the normal procedures the participating institutions and individuals would follow in their own countries.

Receiving institutions of each country will have final approval of students and scholars applying from the other country. Both Parties will, however, use their best efforts to assure the fulfillment of the principles of this accord.

The Parties further agree that the principles of this accord will be the basis of all official educational exchanges. While recognizing the independence of non-official arrangements, the Parties agree these principles should also be extended, to the degree applicable, to the full range of educational exchanges between the two countries.

The Parties will reach detailed agreement on specific programs through regular exchanges of letters or other instruments on at least an annual basis.

Article II — Official Exchanges of Individuals

The Parties agree on the following categories of official exchanges of individuals:

(A) *Research Scholars.* Each Party may select and sponsor scholars from its own country to engage in research in the other country. Each Party may select and sponsor scholars from the other country to engage in research in its own country. Scholars may be placed in association with educational research or other institutions relevant to the accomplishment of research objectives or may, with the approval of the host government, engage in independent research. Research fields will include the humanities, the social sciences, the natural sciences, and the technological sciences.

(B) *Graduate Students.* Each Party may select and sponsor qualified graduates of institutions of higher learning or equivalent of its own country to pursue degree or non-degree graduate programs of study and research in the other country. Each party may select and sponsor qualified graduates of institutions of higher learning or equivalent from the other country to pursue degree or non-degree graduate programs of study and research in its own country. Fields of study will include the humanities, the social sciences, the natural sciences, and the technological sciences.

(C) *Teachers and Lecturers.* The Parties agree to encourage and sponsor teachers, lecturers, professors, and other qualified people of the institutions of higher learning of their respective countries to teach or to give a series of lectures in the other country. Fields of teaching and lecturing will include the humanities, the social sciences, the natural sciences, and the technological sciences.

Article III — Official Delegations and Group Projects

The Parties agree to exchange delegations and groups in various educational fields which may include participation in joint meetings such as conferences and symposia in the areas of mutual interest as agreed.

Article IV — Exchange of Materials

The Parties agree to encourage and facilitate the exchange of scholarly and other educational materials between educational and research institutions of both countries and individuals. Materials may include books, periodicals, monographs, and audiovisual materials.

Article V — Non-official Exchanges

The Parties agree to continue to encourage and promote direct educational exchanges and cooperation between educational organizations, universities, colleges, schools, research institutions, and individuals of their respective countries. The assistance to these exchanges should be facilitated in accordance with each country's laws and regulations.

Article VI — Financial Provisions

(A) The Parties agree that the expenses for official delegations and groups under the auspices of Article III of this accord will be as follows: the sending side shall bear the two-way international travel expenses of the delegation or group. The receiving side shall bear the expenses of board and lodging, transportation, and medical care or health and accident insurance when the delegation or group is in its territory; any exception to these provisions shall be determined by written agreement of the Parties.

(B) The Parties agree that the necessary expenses for the official exchange of individuals under the auspices of Article II of this accord shall be based on the principle that the sending side pays the costs associated with its participants. Exceptions to this principle will be by agreement of the Parties.

(C) The Fulbright and university-to-university affiliation programs and other designated programs shall share certain costs mutually agreed by the Parties and the participating institutions.

(D) The financial provisions for non-official exchanges shall be

169

determined by the participating institutions, the Parties recognizing that public and private institutions of both countries have limited capacity to support educational exchange activities.

(E) The Parties agree that activities under this accord shall be carried out subject to the availability of funds.

Article VII — Executive Agents

(A) The Executive Agent of this accord on the United States side shall be the United States Information Agency. The Executive Agent of this accord on the People's Republic of China side shall be the State Education Commission of the People's Republic of China.

(B) Upon signature, this accord will become part of the official agreements concluded under Article 5 of the Agreement between the Government of the United States of America and the Government of the People's Republic of China on Cooperation in Science and Technology signed January 31, 1979, extended January 12, 1984.

(C) As agreed by the Executive Agents of the Parties, the representatives of agencies or organizations concerned in both countries will exchange visits for the working out of plans and programs of educational exchange and for discussing programs, problems, and matters related to educational exchange projects. These meetings may be held in the United States of America or in the People's Republic of China as agreed.

(D) This accord will supersede the "Understanding on the Exchange of Students between the United States of America and the People's Republic of China" reached in October 1978, and be the guiding document for educational exchanges of the two countries.

This accord shall enter into force upon signature and remain in force for a five-year period. It may be amended or extended by the written agreement of the two Parties; it may be terminated by either Party by giving six months' written notice to the other Party of its intention to terminate.

Done at Washington, this 23rd day of July 1985, in duplicate in the English and Chinese languages, both equally authentic.

For the Government
of the
United States of America:

For the Government
of the
People's Republic of China:

RONALD REAGAN

LI XIANNIAN

Appendix C

Locations and Holdings of U.S. Education Reference Collections in China

Because of limited space and staff, the Press and Cultural Section of the U.S. Embassy, Beijing is unable to handle inquiries regarding study in the United States. For such information, it is suggested that Chinese students and scholars contact one of the organizations listed below. All have materials supplied by the U.S. Embassy, and many of them have persons who have been trained in educational advising.

Beijing Educational Information Center for International Exchange
Beijing Language Institute
15, Xueyuan Lu
Beijing

Study Abroad Training Department
Shanghai International Studies University
Xi Tiyuhui Lu
Shanghai

Study Abroad Information Service
Bureau of Higher Education, Guangdong Province
Xihu Lu
Guangzhou, Guangdong

IIE-Guangdong America Study Information Center
Ground Floor, 46-1 Dezheng Nan Lu
Guangzhou, Guangdong

Study Abroad Training Department
Guangzhou Foreign Lanuages Institute
Beijiao Huangpodong
Guangzhou, Guangdong

Study Abroad Training Center
Sichuan Foreign Languages Department
Shapingba
Chongqing, Sichuan

Study Abroad Training Department
Chengdu University of Science and Technology
Xingnanmenwai Moziqiao
Chengdu, Sichuan

TOEFL Office
Dalian Foreign Languages Institute
Dalian, Liaoning

Study Abroad Training Department
Xi'an Foreign Languages Training Department
Wujiafen
Xi'an, Shaanxi

The following libraries also have materials on study in the United States:

Beijing National Library, Beijing
Guangzhou Municipal Library, Guangzhou, Guangdong
Nanjing Library, Nanjing, Jiangsu
Tianjin Municipal Library, Tianjin
Shanghai Municipal Library, Shanghai
Hebei Provincial Library, Shijiazhuang, Hebei
Henan Provincial Library, Zhengzhou, Henan
Shandong Provincial Library, Jinan, Shandong
Shanxi Provincial Library, Taiyuan, Shanxi
Shaanxi Provincial Library, Xi'an, Shaanxi
Gansu Provincial Library, Lanzhou, Gansu
Hunan Provincial Library, Changsha, Hunan
Hubei Provincial Library, Wuhan, Hubei
Jiangxi Provincial Library, Nanchang, Jiangxi
Sichuan Provincial Library, Chengdu, Sichuan
Guizhou Provincial Library, Guiyang, Guizhou
Fujian Provincial Library, Fuzhou, Fujian
Guangxi Provincial Library, Nanning, Guangxi
Zhejiang Provincial Library, Hangzhou, Zhejiang
Anhui Provincial Libary, Hefei, Anhui
Liaoning Provincial Library, Shenyang, Liaoning
Jilin Provincial Library, Changchun, Jilin
Heilongjiang Provincial Library, Harbin, Heilongjiang

General Reference Works Contained
in the U.S. Education Reference Collections

Accredited Institutions of Postsecondary Education, 1984–85

Accredited Programs Leading to Degrees in Engineering, 1984 (with 1985 addendum)

Accredited Programs Leading to Degrees in Engineering Technology, 1984 (with 1985 addendum)

Adviser's Manual of Federal Regulations Affecting Foreign Students and Scholars (with 1983 emendations)

Allied Health Education Directory, 1985

American Universities and Colleges, 12th edition

The American University—A World Guide

Arrival Information Requests

The College Handbook and Index of Majors (two volumes)

Costs at U.S. Educational Institutions, 1985–86

Directory of Graduate Programs: 1986 and 1987 (four volumes)
  Volume A: Agriculture, Biological Sciences, Psychology, Health Sciences, and Home Economics
  Volume B: Arts and Humanities
  Volume C: Physical Sciences, Mathematics, and Engineering
  Volume D: Social Sciences and Education

Directory of Overseas Educational Advising Centers

Directory of Residency Training Programs, 1985–86

The Doctor of Philosophy Degree

Engineering Education (March 1985 issue: Engineering College Research and Graduate Study)

English Language and Orientation Programs in the United States

Entering Higher Education in the United States—A Guide for Students from Other Countries

Financial Aid Available to Students and Scholars from the People's Republic of China for Study and Research in the United States, 1987

Financial Planning for Study in the United States—A Guide for Students from Other Countries

Foreign Teaching Assistants in U.S. Universities

A Guide to COPA Recognized Accrediting Associations, 1984–86

A Handbook for Foreign Students

Higher Education Directory, 1985

Lovejoy's College Guide, 17th edition

The Master's Degree

Map of Colleges and Universities in the United States

NAFSA (National Association for Foreign Student Affairs) Directory, 1985

NHSC (National Home Study Council) Directory of Home Study Schools, 1985–86

Occupational Outlook Handbook, 1984–85

The Official Guide to MBA Programs, Admissions, and Careers

Open Doors: 1984–85—Report on International Educational Exchange

Peterson's Annual Guides to Graduate Study, 1986 (five volumes)

Graduate and Professional Programs: An Overview (Book 1)

Graduate Programs in the Humanities and Social Sciences (Book 2)

Graduate Programs in the Biological, Agricultural, and Health Sciences (Book 3)

Graduate Programs in the Physical Sciences and Mathematics (Book 4)

Graduate Programs in Engineering and Applied Sciences (Book 5)

Pre-Departure Orientation Handbook for Students from the People's Republic of China Planning to Study in the United States

Profiles: Detailed Analyses of the Foreign Student Population, 1983/84

Specialized Study Options USA

Trade and Technical Careers and Training—Handbook of Accredited Private Trade and Technical Schools

Appendix D

Testing Sites in China for U.S. Standardized Admissions Tests

Preparatory Department, Beijing Language Institute, Beijing.

University of International Business and Economics, Beijing.

*Beijing Institute of Aeronautics and Astronautics, Beijing.

*Foreign Affairs College, Beijing.

*Foreign Languages Department, Beijing Normal University, Beijing.

*Foreign Language Department, Beijing University of Iron and Steel Technology, Beijing.

*Foreign Language Department, Qinghua University, Beijing.

*English Department, Beijing University, Beijing.

*Beijing No. 2 Institute of Foreign Languages, Beijing.

Foreign Language Department, Graduate School of Chinese Academy of Sciences, Beijing.

*Institute of Managerial Cadres of Machines Building Industry, Beijing.

*Beijing Foresty University, Beijing.

*Institute of International Relations, Beijing.

*Beijing International Studies University, Beijing.

Sichuan University, Chengdu.

Preparatory Department, Sichuan Foreign Language Institute, Chongqing.

Preparatory Department, Dalian Foreign Language Institute, Dalian.

Preparatory Department, Guangzhou Foreign Language Institute, Guangzhou.

Hangzhou Institute of Commerce, Hangzhou.

*Hangzhou University, Hangzhou.

University of Heilongjiang, Harbin.

Foreign Language Department, University of Science and Technology of China, Hefei.

Foreign Language Department, Shandong University, Jinan.

Yunnan University, Kunming.

Nanjing University, Nanjing.

Preparatory Department, Shanghai International Studies
 University, 119 Ti Yu Road, West, Shanghai.
*East China Normal University, Shanghai.

Tianjin Bureau of Higher Education, Division of Foreign Affairs,
 Tianjin.

Huazhong Institute of Engineering, Wuhan.
Wuhan University, Wuhan.

College English Department, Xiamen University, Xiamen.

Preparatory Department, Xi'an Foreign Language Institute, Xi'an.

*TOEFL Test Center ONLY

Appendix E

Pinyin Romanization, Pronunciation Guide
to Common Chinese Surnames, and *Pinyin* and
Traditional Names of Provinces
and Major Cities of China

Widespread adoption of *Pinyin*, the system of romanization used in the People's Republic of China, has caused many people to wonder if the pronunciation of familiar (and unfamiliar) words has changed. The answer is no; Chinese characters are pronounced just as they were before foreign-language publications from China and most U.S. publishers switched to *Pinyin* in 1979. What has changed is the way many words are spelled. For example, the system of romanization used by most U.S. publishers before 1979 (the Wade-Giles system) rendered the name of China's former Party Chairman as Mao Tse-tung. His name is pronounced just as before, but now it is spelled Mao Zedong. Similarly, Chou Enlai is now written Zhou Enlai, and Shantung Province is rendered as Shandong.

Additional confusion is caused by the substitution of standard Mandarin names/pronunciation for certain familiar, but erroneous, place-names used previously. Thus, Peking is now correctly rendered as Beijing, and Canton is referred to by its Mandarin pronunciation: Guangzhou.

The switch to *Pinyin* and correct pronunciation of place-names is clearly a case where the explanation of change is more confusing than the change itself, especially for people who are not familiar with previously used romanization systems. To assist those trying to cope with *Pinyin*—and Chinese names—for the first time, the following pages present a simplified guide to the pronunciation of *Pinyin* and the most common Chinese surnames.

Pronunciation Guide to *Pinyin* Romanization

Initials

b	as in baby	k	as in kind	sh	as in shoe
c	as ts in its	l	as in land	t	as in top
ch	as in church	m	as in me	w	as in want
d	as in do	n	as in no	x	as sh in she
f	as in foot	p	as in par	z	as in zero
g	as in go	q	as ch in cheek	zh	as j in jump
h	as in her	r	as in crew		
j	as in jeep	s	as in sister		

Finals

a   as in far

ai   as in aisle

an   as an in can

ang   as ong in gong

ao   as au in sauerkraut

e   as uh in huh or the e in her

ei   as in eight

en   as in chicken

eng   as ung in lung

i   as in machine or ea in eat
as in sir in syllables beginning with c, ch, r, s, sh, z, or zh

iao   as yow in yowl

ian   as i in machine followed by en in chicken

iang   as i in machine followed by ong in gong

ie   as ye in ye

in   as ine in machine

ing   as in sing

iong   as i in machine followed by ong in song

iu   as i in machine followed by o in go

o   as aw in law

ong   as ung in the German pronunciation of jung

ou   as in soul

u   as in rule or as the German ü in ¨uber

ua   as wa in wander

uai   as wi in wide

uan   as ua in guava followed by en in chicken

uang   as ua in guava followed by ng in song

ue   as u in rule followed by e in epsom

ui   as ay in way

un   as in under

uo   as wa in waltz

178

Pronunciation Guide
to Common Chinese Surnames

Pinyin Spelling	Sounds Like	Rhymes With
Ai	eye	high
An	an	can
Bao	bow	cow
Bo	b + awe	raw
Cai	ts (its) + eye	high
Cao	ts (its) + ow (how)	cow
Chang	ch (cheap) + ong	gong
Chen	ch + un	gun
Cheng	ch + ung	lung
Dai	die	high
Deng	dung	lung
Ding	ding	ring
Dong	d + oong	jung (German)
Du	do	you
Duan	du + on	con
Fan	f + an	can
Fang	f + ong	gong
Feng	f + ung	lung
Fu	foo	you
Gan	g + an	can
Gao	g + ow (how)	cow
Gong	g + oong	jung (German)
Guan	gua (guava) + on	can
Gu	goo	you
Guo	gu + awe	raw
Han	h + an	can
He	h + uh	duh
Hong	h + oong	jung (German)
Hu	who	you
Hua	hw + ah	fa
Huang	hw + ong	gong
Ji	gee	knee
Jiang	gee + ong	gong
Jin	Jean	mean
Kang	k + ong	gong
Lin	lean	mean
Liu	lee + owe	owe
Lu	Lou	you

Pinyin Spelling	Sounds Like	Rhymes With
Luo	lu + awe	raw
Ma	ma	fa
Mao	m + ow (how)	cow
Ni	knee	knee
Peng	p + ung	lung
Qi	ch + ee (cheese)	knee
Qian	ch + ee + en (cheese + en)	men
Qiu	ch + ee + owe	owe
Ren	wren	men
Rong	r + oong	jung (German)
Shao	sh + ow (shower)	cow
Shen	shun	run
Shi	New Hampshire	sir
Song	s + oong	jung (German)
Su	Sue	you
Sun	s + un (hund or mund - German)	hund or unter (German)
Tang	t + ong	gong
Wang	w + ong	gong
Wei	weigh	day
Wu	woo	you
Xia	she + ah	ah
Xiao	she + ow	cow
Xie	she + yeah	yeah
Xu	shoe	you
Yan	y + an (tan)	man
Yang	y + ong	gong
Ye	yeah	yeah
Yu	y + u (über - German)	chew
Yuan	yu + an	can
Zeng	dz + ung	lung
Zhang	j + ong	gong
Zhao	j + ow	cow
Zheng	j + ung	lung
Zhong	j + oong	jung (German)
Zhou	Joe	show
Zhu	Jew	you

Pinyin and Traditional Names of
Provinces and Major Cities of China

Provinces, Autonomous Regions (AR),
and Centrally Administered Cities

Pinyin	Traditional	*Pinyin*	Traditional
Anhui	Anhwei	Liaoning	Liaoning
Beijing	Peking	Nei Monggol AR	Inner Mongolia
Fujian	Fukien	Ningxia	Ningsia
Gansu	Kansu	Qinghai	Tsinghai
Guangdong	Kwangtung	Shaanxi	Shensi
Guangxi AR	Kwangsi	Shandong	Shantung
Guizhou	Kweichow	Shanghai	Shanghai
Hebei	Hopeh	Shanxi	Shansi
Heilongjiang	Heilungkiang	Sichuan	Szechuan
Henan	Honan	Tianjin	Tientsin
Hubei	Hupeh	Xinjiang AR	Sinkiang
Hunan	Hunan	Xizang AR	Tibet
Jiangsu	Kiangsu	Yunnan	Yunnan
Jiangxi	Kiangsi	Zhejiang	Chekiang
Jilin	Kirin		

Selected Major Cities

Pinyin	Traditional	*Pinyin*	Traditional
Baotou	Paotow	Nanjing	Nanking
Chengdu	Chengtu	Qingdao	Tsingtao
Chongqing	Chungking	Qiqihar	Tsitsihar
Dalian	Dairen	Shenyang	Mukden
Fuzhou	Foochow	Shijiazhuang	Shih-chia-chuang
Guangzhou	Canton	Suzhou	Soochow
Guiyang	Kweiyang	Urumqi	Urumchi
Hangzhou	Hangchow	Xiamen	Amoy
Hefei	Hofei	Xi'an	Sian
Jinan	Tsinan	Zhengzhou	Cheng-chou
Lanzhou	Lanchow		

Appendix F

Map of China

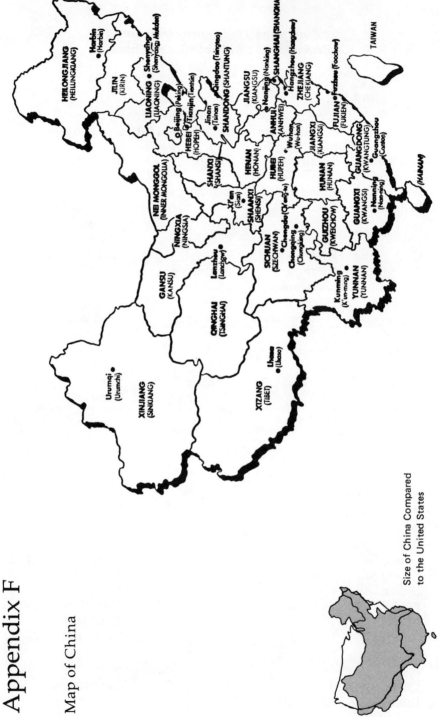

Size of China Compared
to the United States

Appendix G

U.S. Embassy and Consulates in China

U.S. Embassy
Address: Xiushui Bei Jie #3
             Beijing, PRC
Telephone: 52-3831

Ambassador	Winston Lord
Deputy Chief of Mission	Peter Tomsen
Political Counselor	Raymond Burkhardt
Economic Counselor	Kent Weidemann
Commercial Counselor	Richard Johnston
Agricultural Attache	David Schoonover
Science Attache	Pierre Perrolle

U.S. Information Agency (USIA)
   Telephone: 52-1161

Public Affairs Officer	McKinney Russell
Deputy Public Affairs Officer	George Beasley
Cultural Affairs Officer/Academic Adviser	Patrick J. Corcoran
Information Officer	Sylvia Rifkin

U.S. Consulate General/Chengdu
Address: Jinjiang Hotel
             180 Renmin Nan Lu
             Chengdu, PRC
Telephone: 28-24481

Consul General	William Thomas
Branch Public Affairs Officer	Vallerie Steenson

U.S. Consulate General/Guangzhou (Canton)
Address: Dongfang Hotel
             Renmin Bei Lu
             Guangzhou, PRC
Telephone: 66-9900; 67-7702 x 1000

Consul General	Mark Pratt
Branch Public Affairs Officer (USIA)	Daryl Daniels

U.S. Consulate General/Shanghai
Address: 1469 Huaihai Zhong Lu
             Shanghai, PRC
Telephone: 37-9880

Consul General	Charles Sylvester
Branch Public Affairs Officer (USIA)	William Palmer

U.S. Consulate General/Shenyang
Address: 40 Lane 4, Section 5
             Sanjing Lu
             Heping District
             Shenyang, Liaoning PRC
Telephone: 29-0045, 0034, 0054

Consul General	Eugene Dorris
Branch Public Affairs Officer (USIA)	William G. Crowell
Commercial Officer	Barbara Slawecki

Appendix H

Chinese Embassy and Consulates in the United States

Embassy of the People's Republic of China
2300 Connecticut Avenue, N.W.
Washington, DC 20008
Commercial: 202/328-2520
Education: 202/328-2535
Visas: 202/328-2517
Telex: 440038 PRC UI
Commercial: 440673

Consulate General of the People's Republic of China/Chicago
104 South Michigan Avenue, Suite 1200
Chicago, IL 60603
General: 312/346-0287

Consulate General of the People's Republic of China/Houston
3417 Montrose Boulevard
Houston, TX 77006
Commercial: 713/524-4064
General: 713/524-0778
Visas: 713/524-4311
Telex: 762173 chinconsul hou

Consulate General of the People's Republic of China/New York
520 12th Avenue
New York, NY 10036
Commercial: 212/564-1139
Education: 212/279-4260
Visas: 212/279-0885
Telex: 429134 cgcny

Consulate General of the People's Republic of China/San Francisco
1450 Laguna Avenue
San Francisco, CA 94115
Commercial: 415/563-4858
General: 415/563-4885
Visas: 415/563-4857
Telex: 340515 chimission sfo

Appendix I

Pre-Authorization Request Form

TO: Ms. Eleanor J. Harris   DATE:
Visa Services, Coordination
Division
CA/VO/L/C, Room 1343
Department of State
Washington, DC 20520

FROM:

SUBJECT: Request that Pre-Authorization (Notification) be sent
to a U.S. Embassy or Consulate that a foreign national
will be applying for a visa to return to the United
States

The following foreign national is traveling outside the United States
to a third country for a brief period and will need to apply for a new
visa to return. I would appreciate your office notifying the U.S.
Embassy or Consulate indicated below so that the visa application
may be processed expeditiously.

NAME:_____SEX:_____

DATE OF BIRTH:_____PLACE OF BIRTH:_____

OCCUPATION IN HOME COUNTRY:_____

EMPLOYER IN HOME COUNTRY:_____

PURPOSE OF VISIT TO FOREIGN COUNTRY:_____

_____

DATE OF DEPARTURE FROM U.S.:_____DATE OF
RETURN TO U.S._____

U.S. EMBASSY/CONSULATE IN THE FOREIGN COUNTRY
WHERE APPLICANT WILL APPLY FOR THE NEW U.S.VISA:_____

ADDRESS (when appropriate) IN THE U.S. OF THE FOREIGN
EMBASSY/CONSULATE OF THE COUNTRY THE ABOVE-NAMED
PERSON WISHES TO VISIT:_____

_____

LENGTH OF STAY IN U.S. UPON HIS/HER RETURN TO THE U.S.:

_____

ATTACHMENTS:
1. Photocopy of expired U.S. visa
2. Photocopy of Form I-94
3. Photocopy of IAP-66, I-20, or I-171C
4. Letter (when appropriate) from U.S. company

Appendix J

Principal Organizations Working in Specific Areas of U.S.-China Relations

Center for U.S.-China Arts Exchange

423 West 118th Street, Room 1-E

New York, NY 10027

212/280-4648

Concerned primarily with the performing arts, the center facilitates the exchange of materials and performing artists.

China Council of the Asia Society

725 Park Avenue

New York, NY 10021

212/288-6400

The China Council works primarily in the area of public education through its publications and activities sponsored by regional councils throughout the United States.

Committee on Scholarly Communication with the People's Republic of China

National Academy of Sciences

2101 Constitution Avenue, N.W.

Washington, DC 20418

202/334-2718

The Committee on Scholarly Communication with the People's Republic of China (CSCPRC) administers the National Program for Advanced Study and Research in China and plays a major role in other national exchange activities. The CSCPRC is sponsored jointly by the American Council of Learned Societies, the National Academy of Sciences, and the Social Science Research Council.

National Association for Foreign Student Affairs
1860 19th Street, N.W.
Washington, DC 20009
202/462-4811

The National Association for Foreign Student Affairs (NAFSA) is an organization of almost 7,000 institutional and individual members representing the majority of U.S. colleges and universities that enroll foreign students, public and private educational agencies, professional associations, national and international corporations and foundations, and community organizations. It monitors U.S.-China educational exchange activities through a special panel.

National Committee on U.S.-China Relations
777 United Nations Plaza, Room 9B
New York, NY 10017
212/922-1385

The National Committee is the principal national organization working in the area of cultural and civic exchanges.

United States-China Business Council
1818 N Street, N.W., Suite 500
Washington, DC 20036
202/429-0340

The Business Council works to promote U.S.-China trade through technical seminars in China and the United States and a variety of services provided to member companies.

U.S.-China Peoples Friendship Association
110 Maryland Avenue, N.E.
Washington, DC 20002
202/544-7010

The Friendship Association, a national organization with many local branches, is a private organization devoted to improving relations between the Chinese and American people.

Appendix K

Selected Reading List

General

Bonavia, D. *The Chinese*. New York: Lippincott, 1980.

Congressional Quarterly. *China: U.S. Policy Since 1945*. Washington, DC: Congressional Quarterly, 1980.

Fairbank, J.K. *The United States and China*. 4th ed. Cambridge, MA: Harvard University Press, 1979.

Fraser, J. *The Chinese: Portrait of a People*. New York: Summit Books, 1980.

Frolic, M.B. *Mao's People*. Cambridge, MA: Harvard University Press, 1980.

Hinton, H.C., ed. *The People's Republic of China: A Handbook*. Boulder, CO: Westview, 1980.

Hooper, B. *Inside Peking: A Personal Report*. London: MacDonald and Jane's, 1979.

Kaplan, F.M., J.M. Sobin, and S. Andors. *Encyclopedia of China Today*. New York: Harper and Row, 1979.

Kapp, R.A. *Communicating with China: Five Perspectives*. Washington, DC: The China Council of the Asia Society, 1981.

Lo, R.E., and K.S. Kinderman. *In the Eye of the Typhoon*. New York: Harcourt Brace Jovanovich, Inc., 1980.

Matthews, Jay, and Linda Matthews. *One Billion: A China Chronicle*. New York: Random House, 1983.

Meisner, M. *Mao's China: A History of the People's Republic*. New York: Free Press, 1977.

Oxnam, Robert B., and Richard C. Bush, eds. *China Briefing 1981*. Boulder, CO: Westview, 1981.

Salzman, Mark. *Iron and Silk*. New York: Random House, 1987.

Schwarz, Vera. *Long Road Home: A China Journal*. New Haven, CT: Yale University Press, 1984.

Shell, O. *Watch Out for the Foreign Guests*. New York: Pantheon, 1980.

Terrill, R., ed. *The China Difference*. New York: Harper and Row, 1979.

Townsend, J.R., and R.C. Bush, eds. *The People's Republic of China: A Basic Handbook*. New York: The China Council of the Asia Society and the Council on International and Public Affairs, 1981.

Yue, Daiyun, and Carolyn Wakeman. *To the Storm: The Odyssey of a*

Revolutionary Chinese Woman. Berkeley: University of California Press, 1985.

Zongren, Liu. *Two Years in the Melting Pot*. San Francisco: China Books, 1984.

Politics and Economics

Barnett, A.D. *China and the Major Powers in East Asia*. Washington, DC: Brookings Institution, 1977.

Baum, R., ed. *China's Four Modernizations: The New Technological Revolution*. Boulder, CO: Westview, 1980.

Eckstein, A. *China's Economic Revolution*. New York: Cambridge University Press, 1977.

Fingar, T., ed. *China's Quest for Independence: Policy Evolution in the 1970s*. Boulder, CO: Westview, 1980.

Kallgren, J., ed. *The People's Republic of China After Thirty Years: An Overview*. Berkeley, CA: University of California Press, 1979.

Prybyla, J.S. *The Chinese Economy: Problems and Policies*. Columbia, SC: University of South Carolina Press, 1980.

Snow, E. *Red Star Over China*. New York: Vintage Books, 1971.

Townsend, J.R. *Politics in China*. 2d ed. Boston: Little, Brown and Company, 1980.

U.S. Congress, Joint Economic Committee. *Chinese Economy Post-Mao*. Washington, DC: U.S. Government Printing Office, 1978.

Education

Barlow, Tani E., and Donald M. Lowe. *Chinese Reflections: American Teaching in the People's Republic*. New York: Praeger, 1985.

Chen, T.H. *Chinese Education Since 1949*. New York: Pergamon, 1981.

Fingar, T., ed. *Higher Education in the People's Republic of China*. Stanford, CA: Northeast Asia-United States Forum on International Policy, 1980.

Kallgren, Joyce and Simon. *Educational Exchanges: Essays on the Sino-American Experience*. Berkeley, CA: Institute of East Asian Studies, University of California, 1987.

Lampton, David M., with Joyce A. Madancy and Kristen M. Williams for the Committee on Scholarly Communication with the People's Republic of China. *A Relationship Restored: Trends in U.S.-China Educational Exchanges, 1978–84*. Washington, DC: National Academy Press, 1986.

Orleans, L.A. *Chinese Students in America: Policies, Issues and Numbers*. Washington, DC: National Academy Press, 1988.

Pepper, S. "Chinese Education After Mao: Two Steps Forward, Two Steps Back and Begin Again." *China Quarterly*, no. 81 (March 1980): 1–65.

Pepper, S. *China's Universities: Post-Mao Enrollment Policies and Their Impact on the Structure of Secondary Education.* Ann Arbor, MI: Center for Chinese Studies, University of Michigan, 1984.

Shirk, S. "Education Reform and Political Backlash: Recent Changes in Chinese Educational Policy." *Comparative Education Review.* 23, no. 2 (June 1979): 183–217.

Taylor, R. *China's Intellectual Dilemma: Politics and University Enrollment, 1949–1978.* Vancouver: University of British Columbia Press, 1981.

"Teaching in China: What We Give, What We Get." *Asian Survey* 23, no. 11 (November 1983): 1182–1208.

Thurston, Anne F., and Burton Pasternak, eds. *The Social Sciences and Fieldwork in China: Views from the Field.* Boulder, CO: Westview, 1983.

White, D.G. *Party and Professionals: The Political Role of Teachers in Contemporary China.* Armonk, NY: M.E. Sharpe, 1981.

Science

Orleans, L.A., ed. *Science in Contemporary China.* Stanford, CA: Stanford University Press, 1980.

Sigurdson, J. *Technology and Science in the People's Republic of China: An Introduction.* New York: Pergamon, 1980.

Suttmeier, R.P. *Science, Technology, and China's Desire for Modernization.* Stanford, CA: Hoover Institution Press, 1980.

Travel Resources

Customs Hints for Returning U.S. Citizens: Know Before You Go. Washington, DC: U.S. Government Printing Office, 1986.

Garside, Evelyne. *China Companion: A Guide to 100 Cities, Resorts, and Places of Interest in the People's Republic of China.* New York: Farrar, Straus & Giroux, 1981.

General Guidelines on Consular Services. Washington, DC: U.S. Department of State.

A Guide to Living, Studying, and Working in the People's Republic of China and Hong Kong. New Haven, CT: Yale China Association, 1986.

Health Information for International Travel. Washington, DC: U.S. Government Printing Office, 1986.

Henderson, Gail, and Myron Cohen. *The Chinese Hospital: A Socialist Work Unit.* New Haven, CT: Yale University Press, 1984.

Kaplan, Frederick M., and J. Sobin. *Encyclopedia of China Today.* New York: Eurasia Press, 1982.

Kaplan, Frederick M., J. Sobin, and Arne J. de Keijzer. *The China Guidebook.* New York: Eurasia Press, 1986.

Nagel's Encyclopedic Guide to China. Geneva: Nagel Publishers, 1986.

Samagalski, Alan, and Michael Buckley. *China—A Travel Survival Kit.* Berkeley, CA: Lonely Planet, 1985.

Schwarz, Brian. *China Off the Beaten Track*. Hong Kong: St. Martin's Press, 1983.

Turner-Gottschang, Karen, with Linda A. Reed. *China Bound: A Guide to Academic Life and Work in the PRC*. Washington, DC: National Academy Press, 1987.

Appendix L

U.S.-China Education Clearinghouse Publications and NAFSA China Updates, Publications, and Reports

The following two publications produced by the U.S.-China Education Clearinghouse are available from the National Association for Foreign Student Affairs, 1860 19th Street, N.W., Washington, DC 20009.

Assisting Students and Scholars from the People's Republic of China: A Handbook for Community Groups, by Katherine C. Donovan. (1981)

A guide for individuals and community groups assisting PRC citizens in the United States and an aid in developing programs to strengthen ties of friendship and understanding between China and the United States. 53 pp.

Students and Scholars from the People's Republic of China in the United States, August 1981: A Survey Summary, by Thomas Fingar and Linda A. Reed.

A general report of PRC students and scholars in the United States in the academic years 1978–79, 1979–80, and 1980–81, with (then) projections for 1981–82—where they are, what they are studying, who is supporting them financially. 52 pp.

Several other publications on education in the PRC and U.S.-China educational exchanges produced by the clearinghouse are currently out of print. These materials are included in the microfiche system of the Educational Resource Information Center (ERIC) Clearinghouse on Higher Education, a nationwide network sponsored by the National Institute of Education designed to collect and make available educational documents and academic information. Many college and university libraries susbscribe to the ERIC system, and these publications may be available on microfiche locally. To order microfiche copies, contact the ERIC Document Reproduction Service, 3900 Wheeler Avenue, Alexandria, VA 22304.

The following U.S.-China Education Clearinghouse publications are currently available through the ERIC system. Reference numbers are provided for each; these numbers should be used when requesting copies of the publications.

American Study Programs in China: An Interim Report Card, 1982, ED21447

Bound for the United States: An Introduction to U.S. College and University Life, 1982, ED217806

Higher Education and Research in the People's Republic of China: Institutional Profiles, 1982, ED214448

Since the closing of the clearinghouse in 1982, three publications originally produced under its aupsices have been completely revised. They include the present work and the following:

China Bound: A Guide to Academic Life and Work in the PRC, by Karen Turner-Gottschang with Linda A. Reed. (1987)

This publication, produced by the National Academy Press, is a revised version of the 1981 publication *China Bound: A Handbook for American Students, Researchers and Teachers* that was produced by the U.S.-China Education Clearinghouse. It also includes information contained in the NAFSA *Update #1: Teaching in China* and *Update #2: Study in China*. 224 pp. Available from the National Academy Press, 2101 Constitution Avenue, N.W., Washington, DC 20418.

Financial Aid Available to Students and Scholars from the People's Republic of China for Study and Research in the United States, by Linda A. Reed. (1987)

This publication, produced by NAFSA, is a revised and expanded version of the 1981 financial aid publication produced by the U.S.-China Education Clearinghouse. 158 pp. Available from NAFSA.

Since the completion of the clearinghouse's publications, updated information on education in the PRC and U.S.-China educational exchanges has been compiled and is available through a series of *Updates*. The topics of the *Updates*, which are available from NAFSA, are:

Update #3: Administration of U.S. Standardized Admissions Tests in China and Chinese English Language Testing (revised 1986) 11 pp.

Update #4: Television Universities and Spare-Time Universities in China (1984) 5 pp.

Update #5: Profiles of Chinese Postsecondary Institutions (1984) 171 pp.

Update #6: China-U.S. Examination and Application Programs (1984) 12 pp.

List of Specialities in Chinese Universities and Colleges Open to Foreign Students, by the State Education Commission, People's Republic of China. (1986)

This listing, appended to *Update #2: Study in China*, is not included in the revised edition of *China Bound*. 96 pp.

Members of NAFSA were invited to visit the People's Republic of China by the State Education Commission of China in the fall of 1985, the spring of 1986, and the fall of 1987. Ten NAFSA members went on each trip. The following reports summarize the experiences of the delegations and information learned, and present recommendations for other U.S. administrators on U.S.-China educational exchanges.

NAFSA Study Mission to the People's Republic of China, October 14–November 2, 1985 (1986), 47 pp.

NAFSA Study Mission to the People's Republic of China, March 31–April 17, 1986 (1986), 38 pp.

NAFSA Study Mission to the People's Republic of China, October 20–November 3, 1987 (1988), 38 pp.